W9-CLH-816

GHOST HUNTER'S GUIDE

TO

HAUNTED OHIO

CHRIS WOODYARD

Kestrel
Publications

1811 Stonewood Drive
Dayton, OH 45432-4002

EUCLID PUBLIC LIBRARY
631 EAST 222ND STREET
EUCLID, OH 44123
(216) 261-5300

ALSO BY CHRIS WOODYARD
Haunted Ohio: Ghostly Tales from the Buckeye State
Haunted Ohio II: More Ghostly Tales from the Buckeye State
Haunted Ohio III: Still More Ghostly Tales from the Buckeye State
Haunted Ohio IV: Restless Spirits
Spooky Ohio: 13 Traditional Tales
The Wright Stuff: A Guide to Life in the Dayton Area
Star-Spangled Spooks: Tales of Haunted America (in preparation)

Copyright © 2000 Chris Woodyard

All rights reserved. No part of this book may be reproduced or transmitted in any form or by any means, electronic or mechanical, including photocopying, recording, or by any informational storage or retrieval system, including Internet usage—except by a reviewer quoting brief passages in a review—without permission in writing from the publisher. For information contact Kestrel Publications, 1811 Stonewood Drive, Dayton, OH 45432-4002, (937) 426-5110, invisiblei@aol.com.

First Edition, August 2000
Printed in the United States of America
Typesetting by Copy Plus, Dayton, OH
Cover Art by Jessica Wiesel, Columbus, OH and
The Graphic Image, Dayton, OH
Library of Congress Catalog Card Number: 91-75343

Woodyard, Chris
Ghost Hunter's Guide to Haunted Ohio/Chris Woodyard
SUMMARY: A guide to reputedly haunted places open to the public in Ohio.

ISBN: 0962847267
1 Ghosts—Ohio
2 Ohio—Guidebooks
3 Haunted Houses—Ohio
I.Woodyard, Chris II. Title
398.25 W912H
070.593 Wo
Z1033.L73

To Mr. Electromagnetism who cheerfully answers my science questions in words of one syllable.

To Anne Oscard who is always ready to listen over sushi.

To Joye Opt who works tirelessly to make my books look wonderful.

To Linda Marcas, for her encyclopedic stock of useless information.

To Libby Hertenstein, who likes bare-bones ghost stories.

To Marsha Hamilton, for her good sense and ruthless wisdom in the ways of commas.

To Curt Dalton, who makes me look good.

And to my daughter, a treat to go ghost hunting with and to my husband, resident skeptic, technical advisor and devil's advocate, much love.

ACKNOWLEDGMENTS

Thanks to all of the generous people who have contributed their stories and their help. I apologize if I have inadvertently left anyone out.

Kerry Adams, Patterson Homestead; Amy Albrecht; Brenda and Dan Anderson, Old Stone House on the Lake; Pat Appold, Maumee Bay Brewing Company; Tom Burke, Crosskeys Tavern: Louann and Tim Carl, Crosskeys Tavern; Karen Carter, The Golden Lamb; Connie Cartmell, author of *Ghosts of Marietta*; Mary Counts, Briggs Lawrence Co. Public Library; Fred Compton, The Golden Lamb; Richard Crawford, Clermont County Historical Society and author of *Uneasy Spirits: 13 Ghost Stories from Clermont County, Ohio*; Susan Cruse, Promont; Laura Cunningham; Gabrielle Dion, The Taft Museum of Art; Katie Dunn, The Golden Lamb; Pamela Faust, Thurber House; Kim Faris, WGTZ, Z-93; Rick Flynn, Victoria Theatre; Andre Gaccetta, Memorial Hall; David Gaunt, The Golden Lamb; Jay Glenn; "Goatboy," WGTZ, Z-93; Jenny Goe; David Grande, Mid-Ohio Valley Players Theatre; William T. Hall, Central Ohio Fire Museum; Stacey Hann-Ruff, Wood County Historical Center; Angela Harmon, Hopewell Culture National Historical Park; David Hastings, Victoria Theatre; Laurie Hertzel; Gordon Hixon; Rosemary Holderman; Marcia Holmes; Maribelle Hughes, Stagehand's Union, Memorial Hall; Sandy James, Buxton Inn; Joseph Jarzen; Constance Jones, Hopewell Culture National Historical Park; Trish Klei; Dotty Knight, Buxton Inn; Mark Mann, Kelton House; Tina McPhearson, Victoria Theatre; Melanie Mellas; Kayleigh Mellas; Troy and Stacy Murphy; Bonnie Murray, Hopewell Culture National Historical Park; Megan Murray, Hopewell Culture National Historical Park; John Neal, Hopewell Culture National Historical Park; David Offenberger, Mid-Ohio Valley Players Theatre; Mrs. Audrey Orr, Buxton Inn; Julia Pappas, Buxton Inn; Jennifer Pederson, Hopewell Culture National Historical Park; the staff at Punderson Manor House Lodge; Marta Ramey, Briggs Lawrence Co. Public Library; Nick Reiter, The Avalon Foundation; Georgeanne Reuter, Kelton House; Betty Rice, Memorial Hall; Jerri Roberts, The Taft Museum of Art; Janet Rogers, Spitzer House; Scott Schaut, Mansfield Memorial Museum; Deb Scherf; Lori Schillig, The Avalon Foundation; Shelley and Dan Seckel, Ohio State Reformatory Preservation Society; Donna Simmons-Maier; Betty Snider and Scott Snider, Clay Haus; Jeff "Spike" Spears; Carole Spencer, Wood County Historical Center; Taliesin, Taliesin's Boutique of the Unusual; Frank Tesch, Grays Armory; Anne Touvell, Wood County Historical Center; Robert L. Van Der Velde; Anka Vaneff, Oak Hill Cottage; Ike Webb, Ohio State Reformatory Preservation Society; Dr. Larry Welborn; Jim and Shirley Wolf, Stitches in Time Vintage Clothing; Barb Zamlin, North Coast Ghost Tours. A special thanks to the Greene County Library reference staff who cheerfully answered some very strange questions without batting an eye.

TABLE OF CONTENTS

Introduction

INTRODUCTION

That awful primitive terror that has nothing to do with reason or with knowing what you believe in and what you don't.

-Ruth Rendell, *"The Haunting of Shawley Rectory"*-

The great British ghost story writer M.R. James once wrote, "I want to make the reader feel that, 'If I'm not very careful, this could happen to me.'" He set his horrors in settings familiar and comfortable to his listeners, making it all the more plausible that such things could be. In this book you'll also find home-grown horrors, possibly from your own back yard.

I have never gotten used to visiting haunted places, never gotten accustomed to being punched in the stomach by invisible energies. And I've never gotten used to the fear that such places arouse in me. There's no good reason for it—I've only been hurt once by a ghost (*Haunted Ohio III*, p. 44). Ghosts rarely seem conscious of me or of anyone else around them. If they do see the living, they barely take notice, so I have no reason to feel threatened. But something completely primitive takes over when I am in the presence of ghosts, something that tells me to run! Get out of here! I don't know what it is, some hardwired response to flee in the face of the unknown perhaps. I probably should listen but I don't. And this book is the result.

Why a ghostly guide book? In the years I've been writing the *Haunted Ohio* series, I've found that many of my readers are eager to visit haunted sites to attempt to experience a haunting for themselves. Personally you couldn't *pay* me to spend the night in a reputedly haunted place. I rarely sleep well among the dead. But hardly a week passes without a ghost-fan asking me where they can go to see a ghost or to stay in a haunted building.

This book provides those adventurous readers with the information needed to find Ohio's best haunt-spots. Of course, there are no guarantees that you'll see or experience anything. Some people, no matter how eager, simply don't have the ability to see dead people. Yet, sometimes, when someone least expects it, *something* inexplicable will happen. So travel with an open mind. At best, this book provides a passport to the unknown, a map to the seldom-open gateway to the world of spirit. At the very least you'll find a comfortable bed, good food, fascinating stories from Ohio's past, and perhaps a glass of earthly spirits.

Now, a word on "public" vs. "private" property. While you might think that such places as parks, schools, universities, theatres, and movie houses are "public property," there is a difference between being "open to the public" and complete freedom of access to all comers, day or night. I only list sites where the owners/managers have given their permission to be listed. If this ever changes, please respect the owners' wishes and privacy.

A particular word on cemeteries: while a cemetery may be open to the public during certain hours, that doesn't mean that it is public property. Most cemeteries are owned by churches, townships, villages, and other local groups. They may even be on someone's personal land. Many pioneers buried their dead literally in their own back yards. *Never* trespass in cemeteries (or any other area) after dark. There are several good reasons for this:

1.   While you may have the best of ghost-hunting intentions, there are people who haunt cemeteries for less savory purposes. You have more to fear from the living than the dead.

2.   The police routinely haunt cemeteries to discourage vandalism. You don't want to get arrested. "But officer, I was just trying to scare up a spook…" won't impress the law.

3.   Cemeteries can be physically dangerous places. There may be open graves to fall into or flat tombstones hidden in the grass to break a toe on. Confine your visits to the daylight hours. Ghosts can be seen and photographed at all times, day or night. For your own safety make it during the day.

Many people believe that ghosts come out more frequently at night. In truth, I rarely see ghost at night because I make sure I am back at my nice, well-lit, *un*-haunted house *before* it gets dark! At some level we all fear the dark and it is easy to exaggerate fears, sounds, sights and emotions at the midnight hour, which is another good reason not to go ghost-hunting after dark. Another very practical reason is that you might get shot by an irate property owner or even by a crazy person who thought YOU were a ghost. Let's face it, *no* amount of psychic knowledge is worth dying for.

Each chapter of the *Ghost Hunter's Guide to Haunted Ohio* opens with a brief history of the site and its people. Then you'll find the "Haunt History," followed by "Visiting the Site," which lists additional haunt-spots in the area as well as some of my favorite places to eat or visit. If handicapped accessibility is not mentioned for a site, it is not available. The "Directions" section provides an address and phone number, as well as brief directions to the site. I have included the phone numbers *only* for the purpose of calling for hours or directions. Please do not call and ask questions about the ghosts over the phone. Go visit the site and see for yourself.

At the end of this book, in Appendix 1, you'll find a list of Ohio ghost tours to get you started. Appendix 2 gives some useful hints on ghosthunting. Appendix 3 lists other haunt-spots you can visit.

So now sit back, relax, and enjoy your voyage into that terror-tory I call Boo-tiful Ohio. Reread the advice of M.R. James quoted at the beginning of the introduction. And be careful. Be very, very careful....

A note on the photos. These were taken with a Kodak DC290 Zoom digital camera. I know next to nothing about cameras. I point. I shoot. I couldn't fake a double exposure to save my life. So what you see is what showed up. The photos were meant only to show the sites but occasionally anomalies like orbs* showed up in the picture. I find orbs to be about as fascinating and pointless as crop circles. Yes, they seem to be there but what do they *mean?*

A note on names: Names with one asterisk mean that the name was changed 1) by request of the person involved or 2) because I couldn't find the person and ask permission to use their real name. If you are one of these persons and are surprised to see your story here, please contact me.

*Unexplained luminous or transparent balls of light

The Ohio State Reformatory Central Tower

1

ONE THOUSAND SOULS
The Ohio State Reformatory
Mansfield

One thousand cells
One thousand souls
One thousand names
On crime's sad rolls
One thousand schemes that 'ganged aglee'
One thousand slaves that might be free

-Anonymous poem in the Ohio State Reformatory Museum-

The Ohio State Reformatory arises from the low hills around Mansfield like the apparition of a medieval walled city. The ponderous stone construction, tall, arched windows and court-yards stand like the great Cistercian abbeys of Europe. The ecclesiastical motif was no accident: the Ohio State Reformatory was designed by Cleveland architect Levi T. Scofield as a sermon in stone—spiritually uplifting architecture intended to inspire the inmate away from his criminal past to a more elevated way of life.

The Reformatory had been built as an intermediate prison. It served as a stop between the Boys Industrial School in Lancaster and the end of the line, the Ohio Penitentiary in Columbus. The Reformatory's builders were optimistic that the young, mostly first-time offenders were not completely beyond redemption.

The cornerstone was laid on November 4, 1886, "Mansfield's Greatest Day," according to the local newspaper, the *Richland Shield and Banner*. It was the culmination of a long campaign begun shortly after the end of the Civil War to bring the prison to Mansfield. Money problems caused delay after delay and it wasn't until 1896 that the first 150 prisoners were brought by train from Columbus and marched to their cells past a crowd of curious onlookers. Those first inmates were put to work building the prison sewer system, as well as the twenty-five-foot stone wall that surrounded the fifteen-acre complex. The East cell block was not finished until 1908.

The Reformatory, or OSR, was a showplace; local residents would bring visiting friends there to sightsee. The facility was almost entirely self-sufficient, producing enough food to feed all the prison population in Ohio and running its own factories to produce prison uniforms and hand-crafted furniture for government offices. The Superintendent, as the warden was called until 1959, lived with his family in a three-story building at the right front of the property. Prison offices occupied the opposite building.

OSR boasted few famous prisoners. But there were those who gained some measure of fame, or at least notoriety. Henry Baker went on to bigger and badder things as a member of the 1950s Brinks Gang. Gates Brown of Crestline, at OSR from 1958 to 1959 for burglary, later played baseball for the Detroit Tigers. And in 1989, Kevin Mack, a star running back for the Cleveland Browns, served a month at OSR on drug-related charges.

Most inmates served their sentences quietly and anonymously. There were no Birdmen of Mansfield, no Al Capones, no Hannibal Lectors behind these walls. But OSR still had its horror stories. In July of 1948, two former OSR inmates, ironically released for "good behavior," went on a two-week rampage during which six people died. Robert Daniels and John West, dubbed the "mad-dog killers" by the press, first murdered Earl Ambrose, a tavern owner in Columbus. Stealing a car, they then kidnapped the OSR farm superintendent, John Niebel, Niebel's wife and their twenty-year-old daughter and murdered all three in a cornfield off Fleming Falls Road. The next day the ex-cons killed a farmer from Tiffin, out for the evening with his new bride who escaped. Just hours later West shot a truck driver. Two days later, the fugitives were trapped at a roadblock near Van Wert. West died in a shoot-out with police but Daniels was captured. He confessed to the Niebel killings and actually boasted that he expected to die in the electric chair. He did, the following January at the Ohio Penitentiary.

Two correction officers have been murdered in the line of duty at OSR. In 1926, one officer was shot to death at the tower by a former inmate who had returned to break out another prisoner. Another officer died in 1932, beaten to death with a three-foot iron rod while down in the Hole.

"The Hole" was the inmates' name for local control or solitary. Total isolation was a punishment meted out for talking after lights out, refusing to follow orders, or any kind of troublemaking. Sometimes it was inflicted just to break an inmate's spirit. At least one inmate cracked in the silent darkness and hung himself. Another drank poisonous industrial alcohol. In a cruel variation of solitary, two men were placed in a cell designed for one. Only one walked out. The other man, strangled, had been stuffed under a bunk.

Hailed as a model prison when it opened, OSR was criticized for overcrowding and inhumane conditions as early as 1933. Public outcry and a lawsuit forced the closing of the prison in 1990. A new prison, the Mansfield Correctional Institution, was built to replace the Reformatory.

The Ohio State Reformatory has starred in several motion pictures: *Harry and Walter Go to New York, Tango and Cash, Air Force One,* and *The Shawshank Redemption.* The East cell block is listed in the *Guinness Book of World Records* as the world's largest free-standing steel cell block, rising six tiers.

Today, restoration of the prison is ongoing and visitors can view a museum of artifacts, take a fascinating tour of the facility,

A typical cell at the Ohio State Reformatory

and read interviews with former inmates and staff online at the official website at www.mrps.org.

HAUNT HISTORY

The noble medieval architecture of the Ohio State Reformatory was meant to inspire the inmates to a better life. How many of those men left, uplifted in morals and attitude, never to return? And how many other degraded souls still linger?

It was a brilliant fall day in 1998 when I first visited the Reformatory. The autumn leaves of the trees lining the driveway gleamed gold and red. There was a pond next to the driveway. On its banks, I saw a pair of men twisting and wrestling, slipping on the grassy slope. One of the men got the drop on the other and held his head under the water, while the submerged man's legs kicked futilely in the air. Then the scene disappeared. I got the impression that someone had been found drowned in the pond but it had been wrongly ruled a suicide.

What a great introduction! I thought. Trustee Shelley Wilson met me at what used to be the Guardroom. I had first met Shelley, a slender blonde whirlwind of energy, several years earlier at a book signing in Mansfield and she had worked on getting me to visit the Reformatory ever since.

"I'm sorry," she apologized breathlessly, "but I didn't know there was going to be a camera crew going through today."

She mentioned the name of the anchorperson. I cringed. I knew him and was anxious to avoid him. I just wanted to get on with my visit to the site without noisy interruptions. So for the next hour or so I flitted from room to room, always just a step ahead of the anchor and his cameraman. It rather upset my concentration. Just as soon as I thought I was far enough away, they would come tramping up a stairway, forcing me to flee to another area.

I walked through room after room of peeling paint, chunks of fallen plaster, dead birds and other unsavory debris that I really didn't want to examine too closely. It was a grim, chill place. From time to time I would hear distant voices and I could never tell if they were the anchor and his crew, prisoners from Mansfield Correctional working on the grounds, or prisoners beyond all possibility of parole.

The building I was touring had housed the Superintendent's residence. I prowled cautiously through a ruined suite of rooms, complete with a criminally ugly pink-tiled bathroom with a horrid atmosphere, certain that something terrible lay through the next doorway. Instead, I found a ghostly wimp.

He was a very weedy, very young man, dressed in stiff, square-cut jeans and a blue work shirt. I don't have a clear picture of his face. I only know that he was fair-haired, pale, and spotty. He immediately began to whine at me.

"Take me out of here. *Please* take me with you."

He had a high-pitched, disagreeable voice that rasped unpleasantly through my sinuses.

"You're dead," I told him curtly. "You can leave anytime you want."

It was as if he didn't hear me. He followed me, pleading and whining. I began to get irritated. Whiners irk me and, dead or not, this guy was a world-class whiner.

To get away from him, I went back downstairs and found Shelley and Dan, President of the Mansfield Reformatory Preservation Society. Dan took me to the Chapel which was behind a barred door reached by a steep flight of stairs.

"A mighty fortress," I murmured to myself. To my surprise the Chapel was a large, light and airy room.

"The cell blocks lead directly into the Chapel," Dan had told me, so I marched over to the door on the right. Blocking my way was a very big, very ugly prisoner with a shaved head. He looked like a cartoon caricature of a bully. He was crouched over, his arms outspread, his fingers twitching, as if he was saying, "C'mon, I'll take you on. Let's see how tough you are!"

"Over my dead body," I thought, and fled to the opposite side of the chapel. Through the door, I could see down the darkened cell block, the bars leprous with rust, scabbed with corrosion. I hesitated in the doorway. The catwalks had a fragile look, as if their moorings could part at any time, sending me spinning into the abyss where I might meet the brutish ghost with the bad attitude.

I rejoined Shelley and Dan. I told them of my meeting with the wimpy ghost and it was then that Shelley told me of a domestic tragedy played out at OSR in 1950. On Sunday morning, November 6th, the Superintendent's wife, taking a jewelry box down from a closet shelf, apparently dislodged a loaded gun. The pistol hit the floor and with a terrible and deadly randomness, shot the Superintendent's wife through the left lung. The prison doctor was called and it was he who reconstructed the scene and theorized what had happened. She died the next day in Mansfield General Hospital. The prison doctor, for his assiduous handling of the case, had the new prison hospital named for him the following year.

There were whispers that all was not happy within the Superintendent's household. In fact, some said that a violent quarrel had been overheard that very morning. Divorce would have been a politically fatal step for the Superintendent, a former schoolteacher and political ward boss from Toledo, who had ambitions to be appointed head of all Ohio prisons. The two inmates assigned as houseboys to the Superintendent were nowhere to be found that morning, so there were no witnesses and we will never know the facts. What is known is that, in February 1959, the Superintendent suffered a heart attack and died in his office.

What is less well-known is that tour guides and OSR board members have overheard terrible arguments in the vicinity echoing down these many years. The voices are a man's and a woman's. The words are unintelligible but the mood is unmistakable. The quarrel must have been terrible indeed to persist so long, an echo of rage locked in these silent walls.

After hearing her story of the Superintendent's wife I left Shelley promising to return for another visit, uninterrupted by camera crews.

As I walked towards my car in the crisp, sunny fall afternoon, I wasn't thinking about much of anything except how nice it was to be free and back in the light. Suddenly, the wimpy young inmate was behind me.

"Take me with you!" he pleaded. He jumped, piggy-back, onto my back. He was crying. I could feel his spidery arms around my neck in an awkward, choking embrace.

"Get *off!*" I hissed furiously. "Get *off* of me!" And I tried to shrug him off, twisting this way and that. "You can leave on your own! Get *off* me." He weighed nothing at all, but he was suddenly gone from my shoulders. I rushed to my car and didn't look back. I fervently hoped nobody had seen me struggling with the empty air.

On my second visit, Shelley introduced me and my daughter to Ike Webb, Captain of the Tour Guides. He is a tall man with a snowy crewcut and keen blue eyes. His bearing is erect and still authoritative, although he retired from his job as an officer at OSR in December of 1965. In the photos from his personal scrapbook, Webb is the guard with his hat at a jaunty angle or a smart swagger stick under one arm.

"I started out here on nights in January of 1954," he told us. They'd start new men out on nights, he explained, to get the inmates used to them, then they'd be put on an evening shift leading to the night lock-down and finally to days. "If you just put a man on

Hallway in "The Hole" cell block

days right away, he wouldn't last. He'd have to work his way into it."

Now Ike trains new guides and has restored several cells to their 1930-60s appearance, down to the arrangement of the towels. He also scrapes and paints rusting bars and spends a lot of time alone in the building. When I asked him if he has ever experienced anything unusual, he smiled. "I'm so busy, I wouldn't hear or see anything."

On a bright day in June 2000, Ike led Shelley, my daughter and me into the dark tunnels leading to the Hole. I heard the ghostly moan of doves. It seemed strange to hear living things in this place. Just as we were about to enter the Hole cell block, my daughter turned back abruptly, almost in tears.

"I can't go in there," she said, "I can't."

I walked her back to the museum area and saw her off to the car parked in the sunlight. Later my daughter told me, "I walked into the dark room and suddenly I realized Shelley wasn't going to turn the lights on, that there *weren't* any lights to turn on! I was a little creeped out by that. Then it hit me that there was actually a cell to my left. There were people in it, maybe four or five prisoners. And they were making some sort of racket.

"As I walked in," my daughter continued, "I was on the verge of tears. The whole place was such a sad place and I was scared! 'Do I HAVE to go on?' I thought. I felt like I was a wimp but I just couldn't go on."

There were ten cells above and ten cells below on each side of the Hole. Some light filtered in from glass brick windows, although Ike explained that at night the barred cell doors were covered with a solid door, making the darkness complete. Stalactites of peeling paint and rust trembled from the ceiling. Two cells on the bottom floor of the Hole drew my attention especially. I gestured at them, "I don't like these two cells."

Ike smiled for the first time. He patted the bars. "This is the one where an inmate hung himself in 1955."

While Shelley and Ike remained behind, I explored the Hole cell blocks. There was one cell upstairs that I couldn't even pass. I stuck my camera out with one hand and shot into it at random. As the flash lit up the blackened mattress inside, I fancied I saw a white face and clenched hands. There was little light upstairs and I found myself crunching over indescribable debris in the dark, forcing myself to keep walking past those black holes where spirit hands whispered out between the bars to clutch at my arm. I kept close to the wall. Perhaps it was just my imagination, or the blood pulsing in my ears, but I heard a bell tolling somewhere in the distance.

After the Hole, the regular cell blocks seemed as open as the soaring nave of a cathedral. The East cell block towered above us. The lower cells looked like they had been swept by a fire.

We climbed to the Guardroom whose bars, set between massive marble pillars, wore Gothic curves like a set of organ pipes. Ike gestured at the marble floor.

"This floor was swept and waxed every night at 7:30. Security was the number one priority," he said. "Then discipline. And *then* rehabilitation."

I ventured out onto the long walk outside the cells on the fourth level. Here were the two cells that Ike has restored. Each contained two bunks with coarse blankets, a tiny wooden table with two drawers, a sink and toilet. An inmate's jeans, with a red stripe sewn down each leg so inmates could be readily identified, hung from a bar on the wall. Small, hand-lettered signs with each inmate's name were wired to the cell bars.

Beyond the restored cells, I passed a cell where restoration supplies were stored. I noted some paint and a bottle of turpentine and walked on, my nerves on edge. I knew someone else had died here and I was nervous about hitting the correct cell twice in a row. I began to be overwhelmed by despair. I wanted to throw myself off the platform, only the bars made it impossible. I got to the end of the row and came back, limping badly with exhaustion. I noted the numbers of the cells that made me most uneasy. Ike stood at the end of the catwalk; he seemed miles away. I heard Shelley walking around downstairs and looked down but couldn't see her. The bars on the windows threw shadows like the ribs of a dead creature on the far-away floor.

"Cold, cold, cold," said the doves.

As I walked by the cell with the paint and the turpentine, I noticed that the turpentine was gone. In its place was a can of Rustoleum™. I stopped and leaned closer to see what could have

The Ohio State Reformatory East cell block

caused me to mistake a squat can of Rustoleum™ for a glass bottle marked "turpentine." Apparently nothing.

I pointed out the cells I most disliked but, as I had feared, I was way off the mark. Ike counted his way to a cell about midpoint. "This is where an inmate burned himself to death. By the time we could get up here and get the cell open, he was dead."

"How did he do it?" I asked in horror.

"Soaked himself in lighter fluid and paint thinner. The inmates would steal it from the furniture shop and take it back to their cells to sniff."

Paint thinner. Turpentine? I shook my head. Why did I not pick up such a traumatic death, yet somehow managed to see paint thinner? It didn't make any sense.

"He's buried out back in the prison cemetery," Ike said. "His folks wouldn't have anything to do with him."

We found Shelley in the Guardroom.

"Were you walking around down below?" I asked Shelley remembering the footsteps I had heard earlier.

"No, I've been in the Guardroom the whole time," she said.

Shelley kindly went to collect my daughter so she could see the Superintendent's house and the Chapel. Nick Reiter and his partner Lori Schillig of the Avalon Foundation found the Chapel to be a very active area of the prison.

They left a tape recorder running in the Chapel and later heard a mysterious noise on the tape, like a fingernail tapping on the recorder itself.[1]

Shelley returned, bringing my daughter who was more composed now that we were away from the Hole. She was still a bit jumpy though and, I confess, so was I. We peered into the cell blocks from both sides of the Chapel and took a few photos. I kept seeing a figure standing at the top of the stairs to the Chapel and thought it was Ike. Then we found him waiting below. He hadn't ever come up the stairs.

Ike took us through the Superintendent's residence and described the comfortable lifestyle the Reformatory head enjoyed, served by houseboys and entertaining distinguished visitors. On this visit, the building was dead, offering no confidences, no secrets, no visions.

As before, I left OSR behind with a feeling of relief. Nothing had tried to follow me this time. The weedy young inmate was nowhere to be found. I brooded on my failure to identify the cell where the inmate burned himself to death. Something of the defeatist attitude of the prisoners clung to me and I shuddered at the thought of the minute traces of ash that could be clinging to my shoes as I walked into the bright sunlight.

The Ohio State Reformatory is an immense structure. In my two visits I had just barely began to understand its secrets. Its massive stone walls, its barred windows, its locked cell blocks were all mute witnesses to the thousands of men who passed through, leaving their mark in blood, in sweat, or in flame. If these walls could talk? I think, perhaps, it is just as well they do not. Some secrets are meant to be kept.

Visiting the site

OSR is usually open Sunday afternoons 1-4 p.m., May-October. Children under age nine are not admitted. Some parts of the building are very scary, even for teens. Groups may tour by reservation. Handicapped accessibility limited to ground floor. There are *lots* of steps. Food and lodging can be found further up Rt. 30. Other area attractions: Richland Carousel Park in downtown Mansfield is the first new handcarved wooden carousel to be built since the early 1930s. Indoors and open year-round, this is a treat for merry-go-round lovers of all ages. 75 N. Main Street, Mansfield, OH 44902, (419) 522-4223. Nearby, Mohican State Park, 3116 State Route 3, Loudonville, Ohio 44842, (419) 994-5125, is a great place to go for bicycling, skiing and canoeing in season. There is antiquing in nearby Bellville.

Some local haunt spots: Oak Hill Cottage (See p. 92), Mansfield Memorial Museum (See p. 153), Brownella Cottage, (*Haunted Ohio*, p. 128), 132 South Union, Galion, OH 44833, (419) 468-9338, and Malabar Farm State Park, 4050 Bromfield Road, Lucas, OH 44843, (419) 892-2784, home of the infamous Ceely Rose who poisoned her entire family, (*Haunted Ohio*, p. 9). The house is not open to the public but Ceely's ghost is said to look out of the second-story windows.

As you drive on Reformatory Road to the main gate, keep an eye out for the ghost of Phoebe Wise, local hermit and eccentric. Standing over six feet tall, she dressed in colorful, mismatched clothing and in all the jewelry she could carry.

She was often seen walking into Mansfield from her home on Olivesburg Road close to the Reformatory. Phoebe's father had sold land to the state of Ohio for the new prison. Naturally that meant that Phoebe had hidden a vast treasure of gold and gems somewhere in her modest house. At least that was the reasoning of the bandits who broke into Phoebe's house in the winter of 1891 and tortured her to reveal the treasure's hiding place. They escaped with a diamond ring, a watch, and $350 in cash, only to be arrested after they bragged about their exploits at a local saloon.

Phoebe nearly ended up in prison herself after being stalked by the lovelorn Jacob Kastanowitz. When he came to her door with an axe one winter night, she warned him, "If you touch that door, I'll kill you with the rifle I have in my hands."

"My heart, in case you want to be sure, is four inches above the bottom of the left door panel," bantered Jacob as he raised his ax.

Phoebe fired through the door, then sat all night watching, fearing that the silence outside was only a trick. Morning revealed a dead man on the porch. She took the trolley car to town and turned herself in to the police. There was an arraignment but everyone, including the mayor of Mansfield and the Prosecutor, agreed that Jacob had it coming.

Shelley told me of the woman she and her husband Dan had seen. Dan is also on the OSR Board and is President of the Mansfield Reformatory Preservation Society. It was in 1998, at the end of summer.

"We were at the prison for the Sunday tours and were standing in the driveway. We both saw a woman, all hunched over, walking very, very slowly, almost dragging her feet. She wore lots of layers of clothes, a long black skirt, dark sweater, and a long dark scarf on her head. She was walking up Reformatory Road by the gate, heading towards Rt. 545. We saw her for about thirty seconds. Ike walked out of the door behind us. 'Hey, Ike, look! Do you know her?' He had grown up so close to OSR, we thought he might. When we all looked back, she was gone.

'That was probably Phoebe,' said Ike.

Directions

The Ohio State Reformatory
100 Reformatory Road
Mansfield, OH
(419) 522-2644

Web site: www.mrps.org

I-71 to Rt. 30. West towards Mansfield about five miles. Rt. 545 (Wayne St.) exit. Go left/north onto Rt. 545. Reformatory Road is about 1/16th of a mile on the left.

Promont
Photo by Richard Crawford

2

PHANTOMS AT THE FOLLY
Promont
Milford

All, all are sleeping on the hill.

-Edgar Lee Masters-

Originally dubbed "McGrue's Folly," the Italianate building, meant to suggest a sun-drenched villa in Tuscany, was built between 1865 and 1867 by William G. McGrue. The property was very isolated when McGrue began to build, hence the name—because only a fool would build such an elaborate house out in the middle of nowhere! The house incorporated the latest in technology: it had call bells in every room, running water, argon gas fixtures throughout and a central heating system. The prominent tower served, not only as a status symbol, but as a cooling tower on warm days. McGrue made his money selling mules and supplies to the soldiers at Camp Dennison during the Civil War. But when the War ended, so did his affluence. McGrue's Folly was put up for sale.

John M. Pattison was just a youngster living in Owensville when he fell in love with the house on the hill and vowed that someday it would be his. In 1879, when the young lawyer found that the house would be sold for back taxes, he got his chance. In December of 1879, Pattison married Aletheia Williams, the daughter of a classics professor at Ohio Wesleyan, who scoffed at the vulgar moniker, "McGrue's Folly" and christened the house "Promont" or "On Top of the Mountain." There two daughters, Aletheia and Ernestine, and a son, John, were born. When his wife died in childbirth, Pattison married her sister, Anna Williams.

John M. Pattison was a remarkable and hard-working man. During his long career, he served in the Civil War, taught school, practiced law, edited a law magazine, was head of an insurance company, and served as the elected Eleventh District U.S. Representative from 1891-93. In 1905, Pattison, an honest man in an age of political corruption, was elected Governor of Ohio by a huge margin, the only Democrat to win state office. But the campaign took its toll on his health. He delivered his inaugural address in January, 1906, in a snowstorm, came down with pneumonia, and died in June, 1906, shortly after his fifty-ninth birthday. When he became ill and knew he was dying, he simply asked to be taken home to the house he loved so much. His coffin probably lay in state in Promont's front parlor.

The house was sold after Pattison's death to the Hodges, a wealthy family of tobacco farmers, possibly the first millionaire family in Clermont County, who lived at Promont for 40 years. Henry Hodges died in the house, as did his first wife, Kate, and his second wife Blanche. Then it was owned by John Kirgan, who willed it to the Milford Area Historical Society.

HAUNT HISTORY

As Clermont County Historian Rick Crawford and I drove up to Promont in the late afternoon sun of an April day, I caught a frightening glimpse of the house, looming on its crag above us like Hill House, angular and fortress-like. To my relief, the reality was much pleasanter.

We entered through the back door and walked into what appeared to be a startlingly narrow hall—an illusion caused by much of the hall being taken up by the back of the staircase. A creamy loop of molding framed the vivid red paint of the ceiling and the ruby glass lamps winking in the hall above. As I passed the door to a darkened little parlor, I got a quick glimpse of a desk and a settee in the light from the hall and caught my breath. Something was watching from that darkness.

The thought passed as I was introduced to Susan Cruse, the curator, a small woman in a calico jumper with a cloud of dark, pre-Raphaelite hair. We walked past a grouping of family portraits and photos. There was Anna Pattison, tall and regal, in a creamy, lace-trimmed dress. And Mrs. Kate Hodges, a pale blonde with the stark, haunted face of a woman in an Ingmar Bergman film.

We ended in the entrance hall, beside the original front door. There I saw what early visitors to the house would have seen: the stairs to the second floor, sweeping magnificently up to a stained-glass window high above.

Susan pointed out an unusual feature: the marble "mortgage button" in the stair's newel post. Mortgage papers were kept in the post until the mortgage was paid off. Then the papers (or their ashes) were sealed into the post under the "button." Rick and Susan went upstairs to the library and I began my tour.

To the right of the staircase was the dining room, a delicate fantasy of Chinese wallpaper, a crystal fountain of a chandelier, silver and mirrors shimmering in the sunlight that filtered through the cracks of the tall sea-green shutters. It was like being underwater.

At the left of the staircase was the front parlor with an Italian marble fireplace, a spidery hair wreath in a deep frame, and a chandelier adorned with little brass arrows. All the rooms were shuttered and dark, to preserve the furniture, art work, and textiles. The first-floor ceilings are unusually tall, over thirteen feet high, and still boast their original European wedding-cake plaster moldings. Behind this front parlor, where weddings would have been celebrated and the dead laid in their coffins, was a smaller back parlor which, as Susan told me later, would have been used as a "family room."

This was the darkened room I had glimpsed as I first entered the house. I stepped past the pocket doors. The light from the hall just barely lit one corner of the room. Immediately I ran into an invisible barrier, bringing me up short. The same presence that had watched me before through the dark doorway was in the corner, radiating a single word, "DON'T."

I can take a hint. Holding up placatory hands, I backed away.

"I'm going," I said, "I'm going."

I eased myself back out of the dark room through the front parlor and into the hall. It wasn't so much a threatening presence as a stern and disapproving one. I'm not sure what it was but I got the feeling it thought I was being frivolous and didn't want me investigating the back parlor. It seemed to have a masculine energy but could just as easily been a domineering woman.

Shivering, I heard Rick and Susan talking upstairs. I climbed the stairway. It was very like the one in *Psycho*. A slip would have been so easy. Normally I am unafraid of heights but Susan had to encourage me up the beautifully proportioned steps spiraling into the tower.

Back parlor at Promont

I was struck by vertigo on the third-floor landing. The door leading out of the stairwell to the third floor was padlocked. Irrationally, I wanted to bang on it until it opened. I desperately needed to get in, away from the stairs going up and up forever.

I went higher. The walls became dirtier, the paint on the stairs more worn. At the top was a small square room of windows, each side with a tiny balcony. It looked like the pilot house of a ship, with the waves of trees plunging beneath her. I wondered what it would be like to be up in this glass box in a lightning storm. I caught a sudden glimpse of a young boy, cowering as lightning flashed, then being carried unceremoniously down the stairs under some adult's arm. Susan later told me that Pattison had a desk in the tower where he wrote his speeches.

I carefully moved my notebook and camera to my left arm, leaving my right hand free to clutch at the railing as I made my way back to the third-floor landing where Susan waited.

"Would you like to see the third floor?" She opened the door to a broad, barrel-vaulted hall lit at the opposite end by a round window. The walls were a smeary grey where someone had attempted to wash away the grime of decades. Susan pointed out a zinc cistern, the size of a minor swimming pool, one of two that had collected water for the household's use. It was topped by an upside-down billiard table and a wicker casket. The third floor housed the servants' rooms and is now used for storage. One room was full of rotten plaster and ancient, peeling flowered wallpapers. It is in grim contrast to the beauty downstairs and a tribute to the hard work that has gone into the restoration of this house. One unusual feature of Promont is that it was constantly lived in. It was not allowed to decay into a Bates Motel horror on the hill, although said Susan ruefully, "the last owner painted *everything*."

We descended to the second floor. At the front of the house, one bedroom was arranged as a child's room with a rope-strung cannon-ball bed and trundle bed. Displays of tiny clothing, two dolls enjoying a child-size tea party, a scrap screen, made by pasting brightly-colored paper cut-outs onto wood—a Victorian child's diversion—all emphasized the warm charm of this historic home.

Across the hall was the "Master bedroom" with a magnificent half-tester bed. "The previous owner painted it," Susan said, grimacing. "It took two members eighteen months to strip it." The room had its own bath, added in the 1930s, peopled by some unnerving mannequins in ghostly white nightclothes. They were the spookiest thing about the room now, although I was told that Governor Pattison and the last owner of Promont had both died there.

Despite being in the building at all hours, Susan has never experienced anything she would really class as supernatural.

"Oh, there was one thing that happened. Every night I close all the shutters, turn out all the lights, lock the door and set the alarm. The next day, I was the first person back in the house. When I went to open the shutters, I found a shutter in the Master bedroom just *half* open, only one side had been peeled back. If I'm going to open and shut the shutters, I do the whole thing at once. And it couldn't have blown open, they stick and you actually have to lift them." Susan shook her head and laughed. "I don't know…"

However, the volunteers who work at Promont *have* had some odd experiences. Two people were working in the library. Normally a beeping alarm goes off when the back door is opened to alert tour guides. The alarm never went off, yet the pair heard footsteps quietly ascending the stairs. When they peered around the door at the stairs, the sounds stopped. There was no one on the stairs. They

Master bedroom where Governor Pattison died

knew they had left the back door locked and only a few people have keys to the building. They searched the building but found nothing.

Another time, volunteers heard someone moving around in the Master bedroom, the room where Susan noticed the open shutter, the room where Governor Pattison died.

As Rick Crawford reported in his book, *Uneasy Spirits: 13 Ghost Stories from Clermont County, Ohio,* Janet Fryman, a Milford Historical Society volunteer, was sitting in the kitchen with some other volunteers. "We had been cleaning and were sitting in the old kitchen when the girl next to me asked me why I had grabbed her foot, because I was the only one close enough to reach her."[1]

One thing that struck me about the building was how tidy everything was. Susan is very proud of her volunteers who keep Promont so beautifully clean.

"The cleaning people had just finished the first floor and were putting away their cleaning stuff in the kitchen. As they were leaving, they noticed two marks of chewing tobacco spit on the oriental rug in the front parlor." Susan paused and smiled. "Pattison was quite a chewer."

Despite the magnificence of this unique historic house, Promont still has the feel of a much-loved family home. It would have been a cozy haven in winter; a cool retreat in summer. You can almost see the children playing croquet on the lawn while Governor Pattison beams from the verandah. He loved Promont and that love still lingers.

Visiting the site

Only the first floor is handicapped accessible.

Drive by Owensville Village Hall, 115 Main St, US 50. It's the site of the Owensville Historical Society Museum, as well as the Mayor's Court. The building was built in 1859 as the Boston Methodist Episcopal Church. The ghost has been photographed at the big window above the door. Drive by and see if you can see her! See p. 196 for Tours of Haunted Historical Clermont County.

Directions

Promont
906 Main St.
Milford, OH 45150-1767
(513) 248-0324 (call first for hours)

I-275 to State Route 28/Hwy 28, which is Main Street in Milford. Watch for the large Promont sign.

3

GHOSTS AT THE SIGN OF THE GOLDEN LAMB
The Golden Lamb
Lebanon

This quiet Dust was Gentlemen and Ladies,
And Lads and Girls;
Was laughter and ability and sighing,
And frocks and curls.

-Emily Dickinson-

The Golden Lamb began its long and historic life as a two-story log cabin built by Jonas Seaman, who was granted a license in 1803 to operate "a house of public entertainment." Good food and clean linen attracted travelers and the Inn flourished when the Courthouse was built across the street in 1805. To his regret, Seaman found some guests more eager to accept his hospitality than to pay for it, and was finally forced by his mounting debts to sell the Inn. It was bought by Ichabod Corwin, who replaced the log house with a two-story Federal-style brick building in 1815. This building still houses the Golden Lamb's lobby and the second floor above.

Lebanon was a stopover on the stage road to Cincinnati and as coach travel expanded, the Inn grew with it. It also served as an exhibition hall and theatre (the Siamese Twins, Chang and Eng, were an attraction in 1833), a gathering place for lawyers and politicians, a dining hall for public festivals, and a venue for the public bar examinations of law students.

From the Inn's balconies, citizens have cheered the end of six wars and the election of thirty-nine Presidents. The guest registry reads like a nineteenth century *Who's Who*: ten United States Presidents, Charles Dickens, Mark Twain, Henry Clay, Harriet Beecher Stowe, Lord Stanley, later Prime Minister of England, De Witt Clinton, Daniel Webster, and the notorious Clement Laird Vallandigham, dashing lawyer and Copperhead, driven out of Dayton, Ohio for his Southern sympathies. He died a tragicomic

The Golden Lamb

death in 1871 in what is now the Vallandigham Room, demonstrating how one of his legal clients *could* have accidentally shot a man.

In 1926, a young man named Robert H. Jones, trained in hotel management, bought the Inn. He and his wife Virginia held onto it throughout the difficult Depression years, and rebuilt after a fire gutted the top two floors in 1936. After the fire, Robert couldn't afford to refurnish the Inn with new furniture, so he scoured the countryside for what most people regarded as junk. His acquisitions now furnish the fourth-floor museum rooms and include many priceless Shaker pieces. Today the Golden Lamb is a popular restaurant and getaway destination, with each of its guest and dining rooms named for a famous guest from the Inn's rich history.

HAUNT HISTORY

On a raw April day in 1842, English novelist Charles Dickens arrived in a coach from Cincinnati and took dinner at the Inn, then called The Bradley House. Tired and ill-tempered from the last leg of his first American tour, he demanded a drink. Innkeeper Calvin Bradley informed him that the house was a temperance hotel and no alcohol was served. Dickens was outraged and refused to spend the night at the Golden Lamb, recording his annoyance in his *American Notes:* "We dine soon after…and have nothing to drink but tea and coffee. As they are both very bad and the water is worse, I ask for brandy; but it is a temperance hotel, and spirits were not to be had for love or money."[1]

Dickens may have been right about the quality of the tea and coffee, but he was utterly wrong about spirits being unavailable at the Golden Lamb.

"The most famous 'ghost' is the little girl named Sarah," according to Fred Compton, Assistant Manager of the Inn. She was the daughter of Albert and Eunice Stubbs. Albert ran a gristmill in Morrow. He died very young and Eunice and her children moved to the Golden Lamb, managed by Albert's brother Isaac Stubbs Jr. They lived on the second floor of the Inn, where the Presidential Dining Room is today. Sarah and her sister tended the stables to make extra money. "Sarah grew up and had kids and lived to be old," Mr. Compton told me. "But some people think she still haunts the place. I don't buy it," he admitted, speaking of the supposed hauntings. "But I've spoken to people who swear they've had weird things happen."

Tara, who works as a housekeeper, told me, "I get the creeps, especially early in the morning in the winter. It's so bright outside—and so dark inside."

In 1983, two pieces of children's furniture originally owned by Sarah Stubbs were discovered: a rocker and a small table. The owners decided to use them in a museum room full of the artifacts of childhood. It was a charming idea. Workers fitted a glass door to a tiny room on the fourth floor, right next to the stairs. But there was a snag: either guests blocked traffic as they enjoyed the exhibit, or they missed their footing as they glanced into the room on their way down. After several near-accidents, the display was moved

"Sarah's Room"

across the hall to a safer location. It was then that the trouble began.

Shortly after that, the housekeeper said, the maids told her that they kept finding the pictures in the room hanging crooked. They would straighten them, only to find them tilted, often as soon as they turned their back. They also heard the sound of someone stamping ghostly feet in "Sarah's Room"—like a small child throwing a temper tantrum. The maids joked that it was because Sarah was sick and tired of being moved: Her possessions had been moved three times since she had lived there.

I was present for one unexplained incident while visiting the Inn. Just as Mr. Compton was telling me about the pictures in Sarah's Room, a crash sounded in the lobby behind me.

"I was nowhere near that," a young man protested jokingly to his friend. And indeed, there was no one close to the framed picture that had just fallen. The other manager rushed over to replace the picture on its high shelf. I assumed that it had just been propped up on the shelf and had vibrated its way off the edge.

I turned back to Mr. Compton with a ⸱   ⸱ould make something of that," I joked.

Later, as I photographed the framed needlework motto—"No Cross, No Crown—" that fell, I mentioned my "vibrating shelf" idea to David, the manager who had picked up the fallen picture. "Oh no," he said, "the wire holding it snapped." Interesting, I thought, that the wire chose that particular moment to fail, as we were discussing moving pictures.

Today, "Sarah's Room" is on view on the fourth floor. From the wooly lamb on wheels to the sled with swans-heads runners; from the miniature walnut bureau to the tiny domed trunk, the room is a tintype-perfect vision of nineteenth-century childhood.

To the right of the door hang the notorious tilting pictures. Many of them are popular hand-colored prints of girls and young women captioned "Sarah." There is also an old photograph of a lovely young woman with a pair of blonde curls on either side of her forehead. She is wearing the butterfly sleeves of the early 1890s. Below the photo is a copy of its reverse side on which was written in copperplate handwriting: "daughter of Albert and Eunice."

I stamped an experimental foot. The floors seemed to be solid, not visibly slanted. There did not seem to be any overt "bounce" to the floor that might knock pictures askew as guests walked about.

Mr. Compton also told me of some of the untimely deaths at the Golden Lamb and I wondered if the little girl ghost was really Sarah, come back to relive her childhood years, or if she could possibly be Eliza Clay, whose short life ended at the Inn in 1825.

In that summer, statesman Henry Clay, his wife Lucretia, and their youngest daughter, Eliza, were travelling to Washington from their Kentucky home. Eliza, age twelve, was the Clay's only unmarried daughter and her mother was looking forward to having her in Washington to keep her company while Clay was busy with his duties as Secretary of State to President John Quincy Adams. In Cincinnati, Eliza developed a fever. Her parents thought that it was merely excitement over the trip and traveled on to Lebanon where her condition worsened. A local doctor, called to the Golden Lamb, said that she was too sick to be moved. Several weeks passed, and she was no better. Clay was torn between his responsibilities as a husband and father and his position in Washington.

When the doctor assured him that Eliza would recover, Clay decided, with some foreboding, to continue on to Washington. Not twenty miles from the capital, on August 21st, 1825 he read with horror in the *National Intelligencer* that his daughter had died on August 11th. The child was buried in a local cemetery and her body was not brought home to the family's plot in the Lexington Cemetery until the 1890s.[1] One can only imagine the terrible sorrow of Lucretia Clay, forced to bury her dear child among strangers and her melancholy return to Lexington, alone.

It may be this little girl's ghost that several patrons of the Inn saw on a winter's night several years ago. It is the Inn's custom to open the doors of any room not occupied, so that guests can admire the antiques. After dinner, Susan* was exploring the second-floor halls with a group of her friends. Susan was wearing her long fur coat. In the darkness of the wintry evening, the lamps in the rooms glowed softly. As Susan walked down the hall, she felt a small hand stroking her fur coat, as one would pet an animal. Startled, she glanced down. There was a little girl with blonde hair standing there patting the fur with a dreamy expression on her face. Several others in the party saw the little girl also. Then she ran down the passage and simply wasn't there any more.

As I prowled around the Inn, I kept feeling that the little girl was watch-

The pictures in "Sarah's Room" that tilt. Sarah herself is seen in the middle photo at the right.

ing, always from the end of a hall, always just out of sight, stifling her giggles at this game.

There is another, more mature ghost at the Inn: a tall, "grey man." Mr. Compton told me about Ohio Supreme Court Justice Charles R. Sherman, father of General William Tecumseh "Cump" Sherman. Sherman came to Lebanon in 1829 to administer the Bar examination to would-be attorneys, and died almost immediately, somewhere on the second floor. In life, he was a very tall, very thin, grey-looking man. His complexion suggests that something was wrong with his heart. Perhaps it gave out on the stairs that hot June day.

Fifteen years ago, guests began to describe a "gaunt, grey man," particularly in the second-floor hall. One guest felt someone sit down on the bed and thought at first that she was dreaming. When she sat up, she saw a mustached man standing in the room. Her husband spoke to her. She realized that she really was awake. The silent man vanished.

Katie, one of the cleaning staff at the Inn, told me, "I came out of Room 27 on the third floor and smelled cigar smoke. There was nobody on the floor, no guests, nobody. And nobody is allowed to smoke inside the building. I sniffed and thought, 'Who's smoking a cigar?'" No one was there.

Another guest indignantly told the front desk clerk that the ghost had messed with his house slippers! The methodical guest always carefully arranged his slippers by his bed so that he could immediately step into them. When he stayed at the Inn, he heard someone moving around his room. He groped for his slippers in the dark, but never found them. In the morning, the slippers were found by the door, toes neatly pointed inward, as if the ghost had walked them to the door, turned, stepped out of them, and vanished through the door.

Unlike young Sarah Stubbs, Justice Sherman's ghost doesn't have his own room, so he roams the halls. His was another untimely death, leaving much business unfinished. He was only forty-one and left behind a penniless wife and eleven children. When Mrs. Sherman couldn't care for their children, most of the children were reluctantly put out for adoption. Or, with his firm sense of responsibility, the Justice may feel that he failed in his duty and is still trying to administer that 1829 Bar examination.

Of Clement Vallandigham, there is no trace, not even in the room that bears his name, where he accidentally shot himself demonstrating a client's careless handling of a pistol. Perhaps his ghost is simply too embarrassed to haunt.

One thing about the Golden Lamb that has always struck me is its intense quiet. Life seems hushed within its charming rooms and long hallways. Looking out of its wavy glass windows, I wouldn't be surprised to see a dusty dirt road or a torchlight assembly for William Henry Harrison. It is as if the building sits in some nineteenth-century bubble, its thick walls insulating it from the passage of time.

The Inn houses a fascinating collection of Shaker furniture, an important collection of Currier & Ives prints, motto samplers stitched in colorful wools and rare historical artifacts. And, of course, the Inn wouldn't be the Golden Lamb without its hundreds of lamb figurines in all sizes and materials. My favorite was a ghostly wax lamb surrounded by drooping garlands of flowers and foliage captured under a glass dome like a saint's relic.

The Golden Lamb has seen much life, and much untimely death: Eliza Clay; Albert Stubbs and Justice Sherman, who both left behind young families; and Clement Vallandigham, cut off in his prime by a foolish, fatal mistake. Yet it is easy to forget the deaths in the vibrant stream of the living flowing in and out of the dining rooms, stairways and halls. The Inn is a place where the past and present co-exist, where time runs in parallel with our modern world. It takes very little imagination to hear the coach horses stamping and snorting, the jingle of harness, the coarse voices of the ostlers. It takes little imagination to see a small girl in short petticoats, peeping from the end of the halls, in an eternal game of hide and seek.

Visiting the site

The Golden Lamb offers eighteen guest rooms, each with air conditioning, private bath, phone, and television. There are four public and five private dining rooms. The Black Horse Tavern, at the rear of the building, caters to the casual diner, while The Lamb Shop offers gifts and collectibles. Only the first floor is handicapped accessible.

Lebanon allows you to mix ghosthunting and shopping since the town is home to many antique shops and malls, as well as specialty boutiques. Nearby haunt-spots include Waynesville (*Haunted Ohio II*, p. 152), also known for its antique treasures. See p. 198 for the Waynesville Not So Dearly Departed Tour. Glendower State Memorial, a restored 1835 Greek Revival home, 105 Cincinnati Ave., Lebanon, OH, (513) 932-5366. (*Haunted Ohio II:* p. 80) You'll also enjoy visiting The Warren County Historical Society Museum, 105 S Broadway St, Lebanon, OH 45036-1707, (513) 932-1817, with its superb collection of Shaker artifacts. Paramount's Kings Island Park is also close by on I-71.

Directions

The Golden Lamb Inn
27 South Broadway
Lebanon, OH 45036
(513) 932-5065
(513) 621-8373

Web site: www.goldenlamb.com

From Dayton/Toledo:
I-75 to Exit 29 (Monroe-Lebanon Exit) turn East on Route 63. The Inn is approximately 7 miles on the left.

From Cincinnati:
I-71 North to Exit 28 (State Route 48). Bear RIGHT. Follow Rt. 48 North 4 miles to Route 123. Turn LEFT on Rt. 123, The Inn is 1 mile on the RIGHT.

From Columbus:
I-71 South to Exit 32 (Lebanon-Morrow Exit) turn RIGHT on Route 123. The Inn is approximately 4 miles on the right.

PORTRAIT OF A LADY
THE TAFT MUSEUM OF ART
Cincinnati

Every great work of art has two faces, one toward its own time and one toward the future, toward eternity.

-Daniel Barenboim-

One of the oldest surviving wooden structures in Cincinnati, the Museum was built in 1820 by merchant Martin Baum. When he lost his money in a bank panic, the house became a girl's school. In 1829 it was bought by Cincinnati's richest man, Nicholas Longworth. He lived there until 1863, commissioning Robert Scott Duncanson to paint the romantic land- and riverscapes seen in the entrance hall. The house passed through several owners before coming to Anna Sinton Taft, known as "Annie," and her husband Charles Phelps Taft, the half-brother of President William Howard Taft. The couple

The Taft Museum of Art

filled the home with art and music, donating the building and its collections to the people of Cincinnati in 1932.[1]

HAUNT HISTORY

When my daughter was a very young child, museums were my favorite places to visit. Usually we could find some quiet corridor where she could toddle along without disturbing anyone and I could keep my brain from turning into pureed carrots. Monday always seemed to be the day I was most desperate to get out of the house and one of the few museums open on Mondays was the Taft Museum of Art. We spent a lot of time there and I like to think that the Museum has influenced my daughter's interest in the decorative arts. I know it kept me sane.

The Museum's decor is the very essence of refinement with its pale celadon walls and muted satin-and-brocade swags at the windows. On a recent visit, we climbed the stairs under the aristo-cratic gaze of the larger-than-life-size Italian noblewoman in tarnished gold brocade overlooking the stairwell.

A wall-sized case housed a collection of elaborate watches, snuff boxes, and decorative objects glittering with rock crystal and rose diamonds. I strained my eyes to see the oxen no bigger than house-flies on the painted enamel needle cases. A billowy baroque pearl was ingeniously shaped into the body of a tiny dog. Amid these earthly riches sat a sober reminder: a nineteenth-century silver pocket watch with a case shaped like a hydrocephalic skull: a grave *memento mori.*

In a cool, quiet room up the hall hung a collection of portraits: John Singer Sargent's nervous, spidery-fingered Robert Louis Stevenson. Alphonso Taft in chalk-white marble. An Ingres made-moiselle demure in black taffeta and the glittering, rapacious Queen Maria Luisa de Bourbon of Spain, a huge diamond arrow in her coiffure. Further along, in a cheerful yellow room, hung a lively likeness of the rotund William Howard Taft.

Annie and Charles Taft focused their collecting energies on paintings, porcelains and the decorative arts. Some of their acquisi-tions included ninety-seven pieces of Limoges painted enamels, all in half-mourning colors, a curious walnut cupboard carved with grotesque figures, massive Chinese ox-blood vases, and a rock-crystal bowl as transparent as a soap bubble—or a ghost.

When I asked the woman at the gift shop if there were any ghost stories at the Museum, she answered quickly, "We have at least *five* ghosts."

The best known, of course, is Annie Taft.

The following was originally printed in the *Cincinnati Enquirer* in 1991 as "The Fine Art of Haunting" by Owen Findsen. My thanks to them for permission to reprint.

The next time you visit the Taft Museum, remember to say hello to Annie Taft. She died in 1932, but she's still there, some say, protecting her house and art collection. Anna Sinton "Annie" Taft is a ghost.

"Oh yes, Annie's here, and not only Annie. We have a number of ghosts at the Taft," Chief Curator David Torbert Johnson says.

The staff is used to them. They know the ghosts are friendly, though meeting one can send chills up their backs.

Footfalls in the hallway, cold spots, lights moving in the night, the sound of a baby crying. Those are among things reported by staff—and visitors. Sightings too.

"We've had two sightings in the past five years," says Museum Shop Manager Treva Lambing, who vividly recalls an afternoon lawn party, when Katie Laur was playing country music in the museum garden.

"I noticed that one of the security cameras that scan the back of the house was pointing at the ground. There was a guard nearby, and I went over to tell her that the camera was broken. She was looking up at the house and I asked her what she was looking at. 'Oh, Annie,' she said. She was wearing a long pink gown and tapping her foot to the music."

There is no door to the second level balcony where Annie appeared. It is outside the music room, where a portrait of her in a white gown hangs. "I think the security camera pointed down so it wouldn't catch her," Lambing says.

"When I started to work here, I didn't believe in ghosts," Chief of Security John Ring says. "The other guards said I would change my mind when I heard the baby crying and the footsteps in places where no one could be."

Ring has worked at the Taft for almost 20 years, and he has heard the baby, the footsteps and more.

"A few years ago, a guard was working the four-to-midnight shift. His girlfriend was waiting across the street to pick him up. When he came out to the car, she said, 'Did you see me wave at you?' She said she had seen him watching her from the parlor window. The floor is alarmed there. He told her the security guards don't go there at night. But she said, 'I saw you pull back the curtain. You were looking right at me.'"

Annie Taft
Used by permission of The Taft Museum of Art

She was sure it was the figure of a man.

"If it was a man, it could have been David Sinton, Annie's father. He died in the house," says Cate O'Hara, Associate Curator of Public Programs.

How many ghosts haunt the Taft Museum? "I think we have many, many different ghosts," O'Hara says. "It's way too many kinds of things that go on for it to be one ghost."

The house has had a long time to gather a good collection of spirits. It is one of the oldest surviving wooden structures in Cincinnati. Built in 1820 by banker Martin Baum, it became the home of Cincinnati's wealthiest citizen, Nicholas Longworth, between 1829 and 1863.

Industrialist David Sinton purchased the house in 1871 and died there in 1900. His daughter, Anna Sinton Taft, and her husband Charles Phelps Taft, owner and editor of the *Times-Star* and half-brother of President William Howard Taft, filled the home with art before giving the house and the collection to the people of Cincinnati in 1932.

The ghosts appear to be friendly, but people's reactions may not be. Ring recalls, "I was working in the garden one day when these two ladies came running out, a mother and daughter. As they were walking through the building the mother was in the parlor looking at a painting when someone tapped her on the shoulder. She thought it was her daughter but there wasn't anybody in the room. They flew down the steps and out the door. I've never seen anyone so flustered in my life."

Ring has heard footsteps following him down the hall at night, and someone saying, "John."

"I didn't turn around. I just kept walking," he says.

"During a Sunday concert in the music room, people complained of a baby crying. "You could faintly hear it, but there was no baby in the room," Ring says.

The gift shop is haunted, one of the offices is haunted and there is the haunted hallway in the attic, Ring says.

A shop clerk went into the attic one afternoon but could not pass through a hallway because she sensed a presence blocking her way.

"I've never experienced anything like this," Johnson says, "but when I go up to the attic I always say hello and explain what I'm doing up there. If I get to the top of the steps and get a prickly feeling, I go downstairs and come back later when the attic is unoccupied."

The haunted office is now Johnson's. His chair moves more than a foot after the room is locked for the night. There's only one entrance and the window is barred.

Objects fall on the floor in the gift shop.

"We find books and other shop merchandise lying in the middle of the floor," Lambing says.

Ring once saw a book rise off a shelf, move four feet out into the room and drop to the floor, face up.

The ghosts are particularly active when the staff is preparing for an exhibition, Johnson says.

"When the Whistler painting was out of the museum for cleaning, all of our Whistler materials in the shop moved around," Lambing says.

"These are not manifestations of past events," Johnson says. "The ghosts are involved with what we're doing today."

Ring takes no chances. When a new guard is hired, Ring introduces him or her to the portrait of Annie.

Some staff members make it a point to drop by and say hello to Annie every day. After all, it's her house.[2]

I felt Annie Taft's presence most vividly in the music room with its pale gold walls and rows of little gilt chairs. Her portrait hangs there, painted with a vibrancy that suggests she is ready to step out of her frame. Toying with a strand of pearls, she is a creature spun of ice-blue satin and cobwebby lace. A large, luminous pearl hangs from the black velvet band around her throat. She wears a charming smile that made me smile back at her. Her husband, Charles Phelps Taft, has a dashing beard and a twinkle in his eye. They both look as though they enjoyed life immensely.

It may be that the Taft's phantoms continue to enjoy life in the house they loved, among their beloved collections. I can imagine the spirited after-hours parties when all the portraits step out of their frames. Whether their ghosts actually haunt the Taft Museum of Art, the generous spirit of Charles and Annie Taft still lives on.

Visiting the site

Accessible to visitors with mobility impairment. Sensory tours may be scheduled for visitors with visual, auditory, or mental disabilities.

No photography is allowed in the Museum. Also, if you're taking notes use a pencil. Pens are not allowed.

Be sure to visit during the holidays when the building is dressed in its holiday finery.

Other local haunt-spots: Cincinnati Museum of Art, Eden Park Dr, Cincinnati, OH 45202, (513) 721-5204 (*Haunted Ohio III*, p. 76).

Music Hall, 1243 Elm St, Cincinnati, OH 45210-2231, (513) 744-3344 (*Haunted Ohio III*, p.110).

My favorite local eatery is The Montgomery Inn on the Ohio River, 925 Eastern Ave, Cincinnati, OH 45202-1631, (513) 721-7427. Or find a Graeter's Ice Cream store. This local ice cream is uncannily delicious!

Directions

The Taft Museum of Art
316 Pike St
Cincinnati, OH
(513) 241-0343

Web site: www.taftmuseum.org

From any downtown exit, follow Fifth Street east. Turn right on Pike Street. When you turn right on Pike, immediately get in the left lane to enter the Museum. Otherwise you'll end up circling the block. There is limited free parking behind the Museum.

5

AND THEY CALL THE GHOST MARIAH
Clay Haus
Somerset

You may hear the past calling to the future.
-Betty Priest Snider-

Somerset is a small town with a large statue of native son General Philip Sheridan in the town square. The oldest Catholic and the oldest Lutheran churches in Ohio stand in Somerset. The town has a feeling of having been there forever. It was settled early—in 1808—by Pennsylvania Dutch who traveled Zane's Trace, now Somerset's Main Street. Clay Haus was built c. 1812-1820. Zane's

Clay Haus, Somerset

Trace was once about five feet lower to judge by the basement or "keeping room" of Clay Haus, which once stood at street level. Repeated resurfacing has brought the road up to the level we see today. It was in this keeping room long ago that George Jackson, owner of the building, sat down to a meal of venison and wild turkey shot on Big Foot Square, one block west, with his cousin President Andrew Jackson.

In November of 1979, Betty Priest Snider and her husband Carl bought the building. They spent a year renovating the building before opening the Clay Haus Restaurant, naming it for her father, Irwin Clay Priest and "Haus" for her husband's Pennsylvania Dutch heritage. Betty and her children and grandchildren still run the restaurant, a favorite dining tradition in Somerset. Recently they have expanded into the house next door and have created "Zane's Trace Lodgings" on the corner of the block.

HAUNT HISTORY

As I was going through my files, I found a letter from a reader urging me to visit Clay Haus. I made a mental note that it would be a good site to investigate for my next book and then forgot it. It wasn't until I was working my church garage sale that I remembered. Erin Morris, our Youth Minister, was from Somerset. Maybe she'd know something.

"Clay Haus? Sure!" Erin said. "My mother worked there. In fact she helped dig up some of the artifacts on display." She gave me her mother, Rosemary Holderman's phone number and I made an appointment to meet her at Clay Haus for dinner.

Clay Haus is built of warm old brick, baked on the property. The dining room is framed by hand-hewn beams from an old barn. It is crammed with Pennsylvania Dutch antiques, paintings, and local memorabilia. It is a cozy, comfortable room with the feel of sitting down to dinner in a private home.

Owner Betty Snider's grandson greeted us at the door. Then Betty herself came to our table, a slight woman in a shade of periwinkle that suited her silvered pixie hair.

Betty is a remarkable woman. She married at age sixteen, had a number of children, then went back to regular high school to get her diploma at age thirty. She also continued her education by going to college while raising six kids.

"I just came home one day and said to my husband, 'We're buying this building and starting a restaurant. He said, 'You're out of your mind.' But he adjusted," she added with a slight smile.

Rosemary worked at Clay Haus right from the start. She and Betty had been introduced by their minister and "Life's never been the same since!" Rosemary said. "I'm a little out there," she laughed "but I didn't believe in the ghosts at first."

Rosemary became a believer after *something* knocked on the door. She was in the kitchen when there was a firm knocking on the back door which opens to the fire escape. She opened it, but there was nobody there and the fire escape is too high for someone to disappear in the time it took for her to open the door.

As Betty, Rosemary and I talked about their experiences, Betty's son Scott, a lively man with stylish oval glasses and a trim goatee kept materializing tableside whenever he thought of another ghostly detail. He is the chef and manager of the restaurant.

"For me it's just a *feeling*, a presence," he said, pulling up a chair. "It used to terrify me. I wouldn't come in here by myself after closing or after dark. I don't feel that way now. As time goes on, if there *is* a presence, I just catch it out of the corner of my eye. I'll turn to say something to someone standing behind me or watching me from the doorway, but there's no one there. I feel like I'm always dodging spirits walking by at the entrance to the bar. And the weird thing is the activity around here frequently coincides with some special or catastrophic event. The week before a tornado knocked down our barn there was a lot of activity, a scurrying down the stairs."

There was also a flurry of activity for a week or two just before a defective coffee maker caught on fire and gutted the Blue Room exactly at the stroke of midnight on New Year's Eve 1989.

"I thought the firemen were sounding the sirens for the New Year! We had the best-dressed fireman you ever saw." Scott said.

"And there's been a lot of activity this last week," Scott added. "We'll see what happens!" He gestured at his arm. "My hair's standing up just telling you about it!

"If they—the ghosts—*are* here, they've accepted us. In fact they trap us here! It's tough to start up a restaurant. At the beginning if we thought 'I don't want to be doing this any more,' it seemed like they would cause something to happen—like a week of unbelievable business when we really needed it. We stirred the whole building up. They seemed to be so excited about us cleaning it up!"

After dinner, Betty led me downstairs. The keeping room is a charming pioneer-flavored room in the basement with a huge fireplace at one end. It still has its original glass windows as well as the original door with an enormous stone threshold.

"This is where the family did all their living and cooking. We had to dig the keeping room down a foot to meet code. It was all hand dug and the dirt had to be hauled out in a wheelbarrow."

Betty also showed me a case with several shelves of artifacts found when the cellar was dug out: buttons and bits of brightly-painted ceramics, pipe fragments and a shoe meant to fit either a right or left foot. The items date from the 1700s to the 1900s.

One evening about fifteen years ago, Rosemary and Betty were sitting down in the keeping room after hours, alone.

Suddenly, something began to walk down the stairs from the landing.

"I just looked up and saw them coming down those steps," Betty said. Rosemary only saw a triangular-shaped blur, while Betty saw "three distinct people—male, walking down the stairs. Two down, one behind. I looked at them. They stopped with a start and looked at me as if startled to see *us*."

There is a wall cutting off the stair view from where she and Rosemary sat. But she said, "It was like the wall wasn't there or I was looking right *through* the wall!"

Betty described their clothes as dark-colored shirts and pants, "not flashy." They were middle-aged, hatless and had no facial hair.

Rosemary laughed as she remembered their reaction. "Betty looked at me. 'Did you see that?' I looked at her, 'Did you see that?'

"How long did you watch them?" I asked.

"Not long," Betty smiled. "We left. They could still be here for all we know!"

It seems possible. Shortly after that sighting Betty saw a single ghostly man upstairs on the landing near the upstairs dining room called "The Blue Room."

"It looked like one of the three men I saw on the keeping room stairs. I've never forgotten that because it was so *clear*."

Clay Haus stairs

One wonders if the men had anything to do with the case of artifacts. Perhaps they came to look for a lost trouser button, or a favorite old clay pipe.

The stairs seem to be a focal point of activity. Betty said, "You always think you're being brushed by something on the stairs. There are times where running into ghostly people is a daily occurrence!"

Indeed, the Clay Haus seems populated by a number of ghosts, women as well as men.

Betty said, "I was in the kitchen and *she* [the ghost] was in the salad bar room just standing there. She was middle-aged and had dark hair. She was rather heavy, buxom, you might say. And she was wearing a blue plaid dress. I called out, 'Wilma?' thinking it was the cook we had at that time. She saw me and then just faded away.

Rosemary has also seen the buxom belle.

"I saw her through the serving hatch of the kitchen, just her torso from about the neck to the hips. Once she was wearing a blue dress. Another time she had on a pink dress."

If the ghost has a whole ghostly wardrobe, one wonders where she shops?

Not everybody finds the ghosts good company. The Heiner's Bread deliveryman used to have a key to the building. He'd make his rounds at 4 a.m. and restock the Clay Haus pantry before anyone else was up. He would never be specific about what scared him, mentioning only "bangs" and "noises" but he went to the company and told them they'd have to change his route. He was *not* going to be in that building in the dark.

"Things used to fall off the wall. We told this to descendents of the Jackson family who were here on a visit. They said it was probably just Mariah. She lived here around William Jackson's time in the 1850s and was reputed to be part-Shawnee. She was very beautiful but she had quite a temper. She wanted everything just perfect and if she didn't get it, she threw things and broke things. I've heard a rustle and bustle of skirts. I think it's Mariah," said Betty.

Betty told me about a slumber party in the Keeping Room that had been interrupted by Mariah. For the details I contacted Donna Simmons-Maier, the reader who first told me about Clay Haus. She is a friend of Betty's daughter Carla. Later, when I spoke to her by phone, Donna told me, "In 1995, Carla and I spent the Saturday night before Halloween sleeping in front of the hearth of the Clay Haus Tavern Room as kind of a 'girls' night out.' We had pushed all the big tables to the other side of the room and had put the ouija board, which we hadn't used, on one of them. I had had a glass or two or wine and was just lying there, relaxing, wondering when Carla would be back down from the kitchen. Next thing I knew, I got wonked on the head with the ouija board that had been four feet away sitting solidly on a table! 'That's not very nice!' I thought, thinking Carla had done it. I went upstairs and found Carla and Scott in the kitchen. 'Why'd you hit me and run away?' I asked her. Carla denied it. She'd been cleaning the grill the whole time.

Mrs. Snider said the house spirit 'Mariah' was not pleased with our frivolous visit and let me know it!"

"But they are friendly spirits," Betty emphasized. "I think they've learned to live with us....

"Sometimes it's just your destiny," Betty mused. "I went to school to teach school. Instead, I ended up as a waitress and a cook. But it's exciting! You meet a lot of nice people."

At Clay Haus that includes both the living and the dead.

Visiting the site

Clay Haus is known for its hearty country fare. Regulars eagerly await "Baked Steak Night" and "Chicken and Dumplings Night." I enjoyed some of the best mashed potatoes I've ever eaten.

Other area haunt-spots: The Horseshoe Grave, Otterbein Cemetery (*Haunted Ohio III*, p. 153). Take 22W out of Somerset. Turn left on Otterbein Road (there is a sign for Otterbein U.M. Church) The church is about 1/4 mile off 22W. Park at the lot on the side away from the cemetery. Do not go past the church or you will have a long way to go to turn around. The Horseshoe Grave of Mary Angle Henry stands at the furthest corner of the cemetery, surrounded by a little fence. It has been vandalized and is held together by a metal frame, but you can still see the bloody horseshoe on the back of the stone. This is a church burial ground. Please behave reverently, do not touch the gravestones, and do not litter.

Directions

Clay Haus
123 W. Main St
Somerset, OH 43783
(740) 743-1326

70 to Route 13. South to Somerset Exit. Right on Rt. 22, which is West Main Street. Clay Haus is about a block on the left.

"The Horseshoe Grave"

6

THE POOL ROOM
Maumee Bay Brewing Company
Toledo

Death keeps this house of call,
Whose sign-board wears no boast
Save Beds for All.

-Sylvia Townsend Warner, *"East London Cemetery"*-

In the spring of 1859, Toledo was in a fever of excitement about the opening of a fashionable new four-story hostelry: The Oliver House. It was to be a "palace" hotel, with 170 rooms, a ladies' parlor, gentlemen's parlor, billiard room, running water, gas, lights, rosewood furniture, lace curtains, and piano. Almost every single day, from April to June, the Toledo *Blade* printed a puff piece on the wonders of the new hotel: "Good taste characterizes every part of the building, and that this will not be violated we have an earnest in the fine reputation and ample experience of Mr. Baker, the lessee. [the owner of the International House at Niagara Falls]. It is the second Hotel in point of size, and first in point of style in the State of Ohio."[1]

The paper raved about the steam-heated rooms, the "splendid suites of parlors," the million-and-one-quarter bricks that had gone into the building, the artesian wells, and the free omnibus rides to and from the train station.

The site on which the hotel stood had been destined for a courthouse but its owner, Major William Oliver, had visions of a hotel. He began building in 1853 but died shortly afterwards. His son-in-law, James Hall, with partner William R. Morris, finished the work in 1859. Tragically Morris died a few weeks before the hotel's grand opening.

Legend says that Abraham Lincoln stayed one night at Oliver House. By 1894 Oliver House had decayed into a cheap rooming house. Pat Appold bought the building in 1990 and has brought it back to life as a fashionable brew-pub, Maumee Bay Brewing Company.

HAUNT HISTORY

The first time I saw Oliver House in the early 1990s, it frightened me from two blocks away. There was something heavy and foreboding about it, with the sooty color of its uncleaned brick and the desolation of the neighborhood street. Pat Appold has restored the building and turned it into an attractive and popular eatery.

My friend Linda and I went to visit in May 2000. Huge copper tanks and tubing gleamed behind glass framed by hand-hewn beams salvaged from the upper floors. We sat down in the warm brick room with its tall windows, its elaborately mirrored bar and stuffed bison head. The room was pleasant and airy.

We had a lovely lunch. I can enthusiastically recommend the pulled pork sandwich. Linda liked the porter. We chattered away for almost two hours. Before we explored the building, we went into the ladies' room. It was painted a cold, grey-green. I was repulsed by some kind of energy at the end of the room by the handi-

Private dining room at Maumee Bay Brewing Company, formerly the Oliver House lobby

capped stall. Flippantly, Linda blew into it as if to chase it away. I shivered.

After strolling through the dining rooms filled with plants and antiques, we descended into a large oval private dining room, lit by many tall arched windows. This room had been the main lobby of Oliver House. Polished glassware glittered from the walk-in safe, now the bartender's storage pantry. Linda and I took turns guessing where doors and stairways led. It is a most disorienting building. One is never sure where a stairway or hall will lead.

There was a certain silence in the private dining room, as if we were being watched. I poked my nose into what looked like a closet. Some energy batted at my head and I hastily pulled back.

We retraced our steps through the dining areas and walked down the stairs past colorful displays of beer memorabilia to the lower floor. There we found an attractive bar watched over by the "bright tanks" room, another area of the brewery. Through a side doorway to this room I saw a ghostly man in a white apron standing with his back to us.

Just beyond was an empty hall, painted a foul, mottled tangerine color. The atmosphere was jarring after the agreeable rooms upstairs. But it only got worse. We stepped into a darkened pool hall, lit by windows to the outside courtyard. A sunny vision of a couple sharing a drink at a little table outside only made the Pool Hall seem all the darker. I scurried behind a big brick pillar.

"If you stand here and keep your head down," I thought, my heart pounding "they won't see you." I wasn't sure who "they" were.

The atmosphere got worse and worse. My eyesight began to go. Reluctantly I was drawn to the farthest corner, a corner fenced off by a little iron railing, full of a tangle of red-painted pipes and gauges. The rough stone wall was mottled with shrouded shapes.

"The dead corner," I thought.

Behind it, the back of a staircase seemed to seal off a much longer tunnel or passage.

"Where does that go?" Linda wondered out loud. I caught a smell of horrifying corruption and stepped back. Linda smelled nothing. When I told Pat Appold about the malaise in the Pool Room, she did not seem surprised.

"The Dead Corner" of the Pool Room

"That may be why nobody wants to use it," she remarked. "Although I never feel a thing there."

When Pat initially opened the brew-pub, her daughter Cait and son-in-law Matt came to work at the restaurant for the first two years. One evening Cait had stayed late with her husband. She was waiting for him in the private dining room when she heard a man's voice calling her name from beneath the floor, from the then-unfinished Pool Room. It called her three times: "Cait" "Cait" "Cait."

The private dining room and the Pool Room seem to be focal points for the various manifestations. Mrs. Appold told me of the stories she had heard from other people associated with the building.

"Before we started renovations, we put an ad in the paper to sell some cabinets that had come with the building. A man bought four cabinets and when he came back to pick them up he brought a young man to help with the moving."

"The young fellow looked around and said, 'I think I've been here.' He and the other man loaded up the cabinets when all of a sudden the young man said, 'I REMEMBER!' And he wouldn't go back in the building...."

He told Pat that he had been there in the mid-80s when part of the building had been rented out as band rehearsal studios.

"From the drawings we found on the wall, I had a suspicion of what they were into," Pat told me. "You could smell stuff on the street. I don't know if he was just seeing things but he said he saw a woman in a long dress at the top of the stairs leading from the private dining room to the hall with offices off of it. If you were able to come into the room from the street, it would be the right staircase. I tried to get more information out of him, but he was too spooked.

"We renovated a storefront space on the corner of Ottawa Street. Two psychics rented the space. They held consultations and classes and sold really nifty jewelry, incense and other things."

One of the two psychics was Taliesin, who now runs Taliesin's Boutique of the Unusual. (See p. 52)

Taliesin told me, "You should have seen this place in 1994. To get to the bathroom from our shop, it was quite a walk down an ancient hallway past a stairs that went down to the basement. [Note: the stairs are now the elevator shaft.] I had left my store on a wintry Sunday night in 1994 about 9 p.m. I knew there wasn't another soul in the main building. It was always a cold building but that night it seemed *very* cold. As I reached the stairs to the basement, in my peripheral vision I thought I saw the man who was the janitor. I was walking swiftly but I thought that I should probably say 'Hi' to the man. So I turned around. And it WASN'T the janitor.

"I saw someone I called 'The Captain.' I saw a short, very stocky, bandy-legged, and barrel-chested man. He had longish brown hair going gray at the temples. I feel like I got a good look at him. His was a transparent energy; he wasn't as solid as a real man would have been. My first impression was that he was saying, 'I'm glad you noticed me. And I'm happy you're here!' He seemed surprised that I could see him. People had been overlooking this gentleman for many, many years. I blinked and he was gone. I never saw him again. I thought that he was probably the man who built the building. I always felt safe and I always sensed his presence, especially if the building was empty.

Taliesin also knew one of the bricklayers who had fixed up an apartment in the building. "He was a big strapping kid who wasn't afraid of anything," she told me. "He swore he was followed up the stairway. He thought it was nothing at first but when he stopped, the footsteps behind him stopped too. All the way up he heard the footsteps stop and start, stop and start. The stair was well-lit and he couldn't see anything behind him. It shook him up enough that he ran into his room and locked the door."

Joe, one of the managers, says that the private dining room gives people cold chills. Servers have also heard the floorboards creaking in that room. There is also some trouble with doors opening and closing in the private dining room. The door to the "closet" that I stuck my head into opens wide and then closes, as if someone has gone in and out.

Pat told me, "The people in the office say they have had a lot of trouble with the computer. From time to time certain letters will simply not show up on the screen: *Ms* or *Es*, for example. And of course there is 'misplaced stuff.' It can get very annoying.

"Recently one of our servers was tidying up downstairs in the lower pub. She heard a scuffling and looked up to see a chair moving across the room. *She* departed the room."

Pat said, "When we were renovating, I spent a lot of time in the building by myself. In general I felt very protected. I never felt any coldness or negativity."

I agree with her—to a point. While the atmosphere in the upper rooms is very positive and bright, there is that mystifying darkness in the basement.

The trouble is difficult to identify. Pat told me that during the Spanish-American War a trainload of wounded soldiers came through Toledo and were housed at Oliver House for their convalescence. There may well have been deaths among the soldiers. And in Oliver House's sad life as a flophouse, who knows what murders or suicides may have occurred? Untimely demises and unfinished business can create ghosts.

We do not know for certain what deaths occurred here but at least one dead man is buried on the site. The former owner took Pat into an outbuilding and pointed to a remnant of tree trunk sticking up above the cement flooring. To her shock, he told her that a Native American was buried there. When the addition was built in the early 1960s, the bones were uncovered and identified as Native American. Given the cultural climate of that time, the bones were simply re-covered and the garage built over them.

Pat had the building torn down to make way for the front entrance and immediately contacted the local Intertribal Association. "They came and did a sage and tobacco ceremony to put his spirit—they called him "Grandfather"—at ease. We left the tree trunk uncovered as a conduit for his spirit. We're happy we could be respectful of his remains."

For me the Pool Room is rank with decay. Could there be other, unknown burials beneath? Or is it just bad *feng shui*, the Chinese principal of geomancy or placement? Could energy be eddying in a sullen, stagnant pool back in the "dead corner"? Ghostly occurrences have been associated with water and we know there are artesian wells on the site. Could the feeling be banished by something as simple as a dehumidifier? Or is this atmosphere the remnant of some much-older evil, a massacre or a battle? We simply do not know.

I, for one, am looking forward to another visit to this incarnation of Oliver House. I like the food and the quirky decorator touches like the old street signs and the antique furniture. I like the light and delightful dining areas on the upper floor. But I intend to stay well away from the Pool Room.

Visiting the site

Fully handicapped accessible.

Other haunt-spots in the area:

Collingwood Arts Center, 2413 Collingwood Blvd., Toledo, OH 43620-1153, (419) 244-ARTS. This is not open for tours but you can attend classes and theatre performances at the Addams-family-esque site. (*Haunted Ohio III*, p. 185).

The Linck Inn, 301 River Rd., Maumee, OH 43536, (419) 893-2388 (*Haunted Ohio III*, p. 172 described when it was the Chadwick Inn).

Columbian House, 3 N. River Rd., Waterville, OH 43566, (419) 878-3006 (*Haunted Ohio III*, p. 164).

Fort Meigs State Memorial Park, 29100 West River Rd., Perrysburg, OH 43551. See p. 197 for the Garrison Ghost Walk.

Taliesin's Boutique of the Unusual, 4330 Monroe Street, Toledo, OH 43606, (419) 473-2050, a metaphysical arts, crafts, jewelry, and incense store. Taliesin gives a variety of different types of psychic readings. A man was murdered in the office some years back. Taliesin said, "I am very comfortable with [the ghost]. I haven't tried to interact with it. As a professional psychic, I'm used to blocking things out so I don't know if I'm just blocking it out or whether it doesn't feel threatening to me. It made a couple of the people who work here very uncomfortable. They said that there was a feeling of fear and they just wanted out of the office area. One of the doors opens and closes by itself. It may just be residual energies."

Directions

Maumee Bay Brewing Company
27 Broadway
Toledo, OH 43602-1769
(419) 241-1253

I-75 North to Miami Street exit (Rt. 65). Bear right (northeast); turn right on Miami Street. Turn left on Navarre Ave. then right on Miami Street. Turn left onto Woodville Rd. (Hwy 2, West). Turn right onto Ottawa St.

7

BACK! BY POPULAR DEMAND!
Mid-Ohio Valley Players Theatre
Marietta

These our actors,
As I foretold you, were all spirits, and
Are melted into air, into thin air.

-William Shakespeare, *The Tempest*-

There is an indefinable feeling about river towns, a feeling of impermanence, of transience. But Marietta, standing on the banks of the Ohio River, is much more than a river town. It has a solidity, a heritage of gracious nineteenth-century homes and tree-lined streets. Marietta is the kind of town some people never want to leave.

Formerly known as the Ohio Theatre or the Putnam Theatre, Mid-Ohio Valley Players Theatre was built around 1914 in a time of transition. There was a stage for vaudeville as well as a projection

Mid-Ohio Valley Players Theatre

booth for silent movies. The theatre was part of a chain of small vaudeville theatres owned by a Mr. Shea.

HAUNT HISTORY

"Welcome to the Theatre!" said David Offenberger expansively, holding the door open for me. He had a broad, freckled face with smiling, deep-set eyes. He wore a single earring, which gave him the air of a jolly pirate.

Children were flooding into the building for a youth theatre rehearsal and I could see that any quiet Communing with the Infinite was out of the question. I went along with David and enjoyed the tour. The theatre itself is not particularly elaborate but it is obviously well-used and well-loved.

Backstage David gestured upwards, trying to make himself heard over the square-dance music and the hoe-downing children.

"We have the original asbestos curtain and an intricate 'air-cooled' ventilation system, which was hailed as state-of-the-art at the time."

He showed me the Green Room, lit by a single light bulb, then a paint-spattered tool room and the hall outside it, ending in a grubby sink. We climbed to the second floor, walking past dressing rooms with walls of streaky exposed brick and entered a costume room with exquisite vintage pieces hanging on clotheslines. A magenta and black oriental dress dropped abruptly from its hanger onto my head.

"Somebody wants to say 'hi,' David said as I untangled myself.

He swung open a heavy fire door that looked like an entrance to a grave vault. "These fire doors were built to contain the fires that would occur when the projectors caught on fire." Early projectors were lit by highly flammable arc lights like welding rods or sparklers and early nitrate film was unstable and highly flammable as well. Fire was a constant danger in movie houses.

David showed me the prop room, complete with coffin, plastic severed limbs, and a huge furry stuffed spider. Up another flight of stairs was the makeup room. With its pigeon-holes, old-fashioned barber chairs, and mirror-lined walls, the room looked like it came straight out of a 1930s Hollywood musical.

The children were still promenading onstage so David and I adjourned to a local bar to chat about the theatre's haunts. David lit up a cigarette and related his experiences in the best theatrical storytelling tradition.

I've been at the theatre since 1978. I have no title. But I've done everything from cleaning toilets to directing. In volunteer theatre, you do everything!

Everyone hears stories in old theatres. When I heard the stories, I said, "Absolutely *not!* It's an old, spooky building, you're going to hear noises; you're going to scare yourself." At this theatre they call the ghost "Mr. Shea." He owned a string of theatres but I can't imagine that this was his favorite, so why would he be here? I didn't put any stock in it. In fact, I thought, "If that happened to me, I wouldn't tell a soul!" But then I started noticing things...

For example, in the theatre, if you get a good paint brush you hide it! I'd clean my brush, wrap it up in some paper towels and hide it on a window ledge in the bathroom or something. I'd go back the next day and it would be gone. I'd just assume somebody had found it, but then an hour later, there it would be in the same place. Just stupid things like that.

The first show I directed was *The Little Foxes*. Now there's a pivotal scene where the husband, who is in a wheelchair, opens a bottle of medicine and spills it. After opening night, the stage manager was picking up props, but couldn't find the cork to the medicine bottle. She looked everywhere, then decided to get a new cork. The next evening, I moved the wheelchair, shook out the lap robe and folded it. I moved all the furniture on stage, swept and vacuumed, and wiped the table. I put everything back. The show went on the second night. Afterwards I picked up the bottle from the table where it had been dropped during the performance. Fran had the new cork in her hand. I handed her the bottle. We both heard something hit the floor. We looked down and there was the old cork.

We both stood there and looked at the bottle and the cork. Fran said, "I don't even want to know...."

The next show was *Round and Round the Garden*. Part of the set was a little fence. Ginger and I were the only two people in the theatre. I was in the paint room. Ginger was out on stage, chatting away. I came out from the room and said, "Ginger, what are you doing?" She sat straight up, gasping.

"Did I scare you?"

"How did you get over there so fast?" she stammered.

"I've been in the paint room."

"No, you were standing there."

Ginger had seen legs standing beyond the fence and thought that I was standing there watching her.

I just filed this away—as *another* one. I just started watching and listening.

David took a sip of his soda and continued:

My episode came a year or so after I directed *The Little Foxes*, in about 1981 or 1982. We were doing *One Flew Over the Cuckoo's Nest*. Me and two other people were finishing the set late at night. I had every light in the house on because I wanted to see where the shadows fell on the scenery. At 11:30 p.m. my two friends said, "We're out of here. Come on up to our place and hang out."

"No," I said. "I'll finish up and just go." So they packed up. I finished what I was working on and went to turn the furnace off at the top of the stairway going up to the stage. I switched off the blower, turned and took three steps to the sink. For the first time in my life, I felt *somebody* come up behind me. I stopped dead. I got very hot. All the hair stood up on my body.

"It's a breeze," I rationalized. But I noticed that the ropes in front of me were not swinging. Next I thought, "It's a rat!" So I glanced down, expecting to see something scurry by. Instead I felt something brush my shoulder. And at my ear I heard a sigh.

The presence went in front of me then back into the dressing room.

I was completely caught off guard. I truly couldn't move. I looked down at the paint brushes in my hand and thought, "These are old brushes. They don't really need to be cleaned!" And I skipped across the stage and out the door. I got across the bridge, then started shaking. Instead of going home, I went to my friends' house. My friend said, "You look like you saw a ghost!"

To this day, when I'm in there by myself, I don't skip, but I walk quickly and pull the door closed. I don't turn around until it's shut. I don't want to see something standing there watching me leave.

After the sigh incident I swore if it ever happened again, I'd look. Of course, I was curious after I got over the initial shock—two months later! A couple of years later, we were doing *Frankenstein.* I was playing the creature and got in at 5 p.m. to start makeup. I came in the front door and it was so dark in the theatre. I just hated it. I got to the head of the basement stair and had to reach around the door frame in the dark to get to the light switch. I'm always afraid something will touch my hand as I do that. As soon as I switched it on, the bulb shattered and glass showered onto the stairs. I swept it up and said, "I'll repair it later."

So I did the show, went to the after-show party, and was heading for home when I thought, "You know, I didn't turn off the furnace." It was one in the morning and I wasn't thinking about anything except that I was annoyed about the furnace. I went to turn the light on. And, of course, there was no light. I hadn't fixed it. So I brought out my lighter, hit the furnace switch and left. I came back down the stairs by the stage and got the same feeling of something coming up behind me.

Mid-Ohio Valley Players Theatre basement stairs where
David felt "something" behind him

I *physically* couldn't turn around. I just kept moving and it kept moving behind me. About the first row, I could feel it *stop*. I got this weird impression that if I turned, I would see someone with their arms crossed, tapping a toe, as if to say, "Well, what are *you* doing there?"

David chuckled as he said, "I've had my share of stupid things happen. Once I went down into the basement to look for something. The light was always burning out in the storage room. I reached for my trusty lighter, flicked it, and found a face hanging there, just a few inches away from mine."

He paused a beat while I gasped.

"It was a mannequin somebody had moved without telling me!"

But not everything can be explained by misplaced mannequins.

One evening David met a friend of his at the theatre for a play-reading committee meeting. They walked into the theatre together. She sat in one row. He sat in another row in front of her and a little to one side.

"The stage was set with a big bay window with many panels." David told me. "Suddenly my friend said, 'There's something up there!'

"I thought she was trying to spook me. 'Yeah, sure,' I said.

"That is until I saw a figure jumping from the lobby doors, hopping up to the back row of seats, as I turned to speak to her. That's when I moved to the seat in front of her. 'Great!' I thought, 'she says she sees something and now she's got *me* seeing things!'

"Then I dropped a pencil and as I straightened up, she pounded me on the back. 'Do you see that?' she said in a loud whisper.

"A white shape moved across that window. It was a white *thing*. Shapeless, like a long cotton ball. It glided at a casual pace across the window and was lost behind the rest of the set. We just looked at each other. She seemed to be satisfied that I had seen something too and it wasn't just her. My reaction? Well, we waited for the others to show up before we ventured backstage!"

David lit another cigarette and summed up the entire experience. "That's all we've got: a blob, a sigh and a feeling."

The stories about "Mr. Shea" date back to well before David came to MOVP. A lady usher who had worked at the Colony Theatre across the street and the MOVP when it was the Putnam asked David, "Have you see the eyes in the projection booth?"

"Dorothy," David told her, "I *don't* want to hear about this."

She said that as she was closing and turning out the lights, she could see two eyes, looking down from the projection booth."

"When I leave at night, my eyes do *not* go up there." David said firmly. "I don't want to see."

It seems as though the intangible "Mr. Shea" prefers to remain behind the scenes. As told in Connie Cartmell's book, *Ghosts of Marietta*, David Grande, director and longtime supporter of the Players Theatre actually followed the ghost.

"We were painting on stage and I went down to the first row to get something from a duffel bag. I looked up, back toward the lobby, and saw somebody's reflection on the glass, standing in the back of the theatre.

"Thinking a passerby needed help, Grande walked toward the back of the empty theatre.

"I saw a gentleman dressed in a top coat and hat. I could still see the reflection, all the way up the aisle. But as I got very close to the door, the angle changed and I couldn't see the reflection any longer.

"Grande pushed the doors to the lobby open and looked for the man. The lobby was empty. And the outside doors were chained shut." [1]

Dusk was falling as I said goodbye to David Offenberger at the theatre parking lot.

"A lot of people have died on that stage," he mused, looking at the building. Then, as I blinked, he added with expert timing. "In *plays.*"

One of the most unsettling things about the Thing in the Theatre is its sheer unpredictability. It seems to be improvising. One never knows where or when it will pop out of the wings. Perhaps the irregular nature of his appearances has some occult significance. In life, Mr. Shea owned several other theatres. Could it be that the ghostly "Mr. Shea" is simply making the rounds? Or on certain nights, does he have a command performance elsewhere?

Visiting the site

The Theatre is completely handicapped accessible.

I am deeply indebted to Connie Cartmell, author of *Ghosts of Marietta* and the upcoming *Ghosts of the River,* who generously shared her information on the theatre and who took time to take me on a tour of Marietta. I fell in love with this city, so full of quiet, tree-lined streets and beautiful houses.

Things to see and do: First buy a copy of *Ghosts of Marietta.* Connie has mapped out all the best local haunt-spots. Then see what's playing at the Mid-Ohio Valley Players Theatre! Or enjoy an old-fashioned mustache-twirling melodrama at the Showboat Becky Thatcher.

There's a railroad museum, a dollhouse and toy museum, a Coca-Cola museum, the confluence of the Ohio and the Muskingum Rivers, and loads of history within easy driving or walking distance.

I stayed at the Buckley House, a beautiful and quiet B&B with a tragic history: A young Chinese missionary student living at the house fell in love with the German house maid. They pledged their love as husband and wife but his patroness found out and sent the girl away to Cincinnati. When she discovered that the couple was still writing to each other she brought in the local minister to lecture the young man on his sinful behavior. The young man then killed himself with chloroform. His ghost is said to haunt the house but I slept like the dead.

Buckley House

Directions

Mid Ohio Valley Players Theatre
The Mid-Ohio Valley Players Theatre
Third & Putnam Sts.
Marietta, Ohio 45750
(740) 374-9434

Take 77 South to Exit One, to Pike Street, Hwy 7 (West). Turn right on Muskingum Dr. (Hwy 60 NW). Turn left onto Putnam Street. The Theatre is on the right. There's a fancy mural of a former hotel painted on the wall of the parking lot. Not all the parking in the lot is for the theatre, so use caution when parking.

8

ANCESTRAL HAUNTS
Patterson Homestead
Dayton

She considers that a family of such antiquity and
importance has a right to a ghost.

-Charles Dickens, *Bleak House (1853)-*

Since 1804, when Revolutionary War veteran Colonel Robert
Patterson first brought his family to the Miami Valley, the Patterson
family has been as much a part of the Dayton landscape as the
rivers that shaped the city's destiny. Initially Col. Robert and his
wife, Elizabeth, bought 700 acres from Daniel Cooper, one of the
founders of Dayton. Eventually they amassed an estate that encom-
passed over 2,000 acres. On the property, later known as Rubicon

Patterson Homestead

Farm, they built a rather old-fashioned four-room brick house in 1811. It was one room deep, like the houses where they had grown up in Pennsylvania. Patterson farmed and ran two gristmills. In 1821, the Pattersons added a dining room and parlor and two bedrooms above. Col. Robert died in the eight-room house that his son, Jefferson Patterson and his wife Julia, inherited in 1840. The family lived in it until 1868 with nine of their eleven children.

A house of this age has seen much sorrow. In 1863, Jefferson Patterson died in Columbus; a day later, his seventeen-year-old daughter Katie died in Cincinnati. Their double funeral was held at the Patterson Homestead. Jefferson's son William, age twenty-six, died in 1865 at the house of Civil War-related injuries. Daughter Elizabeth, age eight, and son Stewart, sixteen, died there in 1849 and 1868 respectively, probably of typhoid fever. The family suspected that their water was contaminated by the sewage runoff from the insane asylum on Wilmington Pike. This prompted the survivors to move to a new house downtown.

The Patterson descendents—Jefferson and Julia's sons Frank and John, owners of the National Cash Register Company (NCR); Frank's wife, Julia Shaw; and their son, diplomat Jefferson Patterson, had a strong sense of family history and heritage. They wanted to preserve the home to honor the legacy of their pioneering family. The family always maintained the house; always made use of it, whether as a women's dorm for NCR employees or as Julia Johnston Patterson's summer home.

Presented to the City of Dayton in 1953 by Jefferson Patterson, the home continues to illustrate the history of Dayton through the lives of the Pattersons. It is now managed by the Montgomery County Historical Society, and, as Curator Kerry Adams says, "The house is still revealing itself."

HAUNT HISTORY

It was an ordinary, dark October morning in 1998 when my daughter and I pulled up to Patterson Homestead for the Z-93 Halloween remote broadcast. I'd been there before—doing talks or just visiting. It always seemed a warm and friendly kind of haunted house, full of much-loved family spirits who enjoyed watching the living taking care of "their" house.

But this morning something was different. I sensed it as soon as we stepped into the kitchen. Usually a comfortable place where you could chat over a cup of tea, away from the historical formality of the rest of the house, the kitchen seemed darker than usual, with a strange tension in the air. Z-93 morning radio DJ Kim Faris was chatting with my friend, writer and psychic researcher, Anne Oscard and with Kerry Adams, the new curator, whom I was meeting for the first time, an elegant, nervous young man. The three seemed depressed, listless, even sad.

Two men bustled in from the hallway. Sean was tall, dark-haired and bearded. His eyes moved restlessly, giving him a detached, superficial air. I knew the type—the typical morning drive-time DJ—a bit abrasive, only interested in the next gimmick to attract ratings. Goatboy (his radio name) was younger, milder-mannered than Sean, and more conciliatory. It was almost as if they were doing a "Good Cop/Bad Cop" routine—one playing the skeptic, the other the believer.

Sean and Goatboy joked back and forth about ghosts. Sean in particular wanted to "stir something up." He told me later that they had had a lot of trouble getting on air at first. Still, Sean didn't take the hint: "Things that scare me and intimidate me—I go ahead and do them anyway. I was probably more of an instigator than Goatboy. When I was first walking through the house by myself, I thought, 'Well, you know, [the ghosts are] going to have to deal with it.' At the same time I was thinking, 'If there is something here, I really want to be open to it.' I wasn't going to shy away; I really wanted something to happen that would blow me away. I was very aggressive and cocky. Goatboy, on the other hand, was very reverent. But after most of the morning show was over, I started feeling that I had taken the whole situation too lightly. I guess I wanted to test myself and my courage."

Even though I had been told that this would be a live broadcast, I was tired and hadn't anticipated actually walking around the house. So I was a little surprised when Sean beckoned for us to follow them out the door into the hall. Reluctantly I headed for the stairs.

Kim later told me, "When we started up the stairs, Goatboy and I felt a cold rush of air fly by us. Right after that Anne said, 'There's a woman standing against the railing, watching us walk up the stairs.' I was very uncomfortable and said, 'Anne, does she look happy?' 'No,' Anne replied, 'I don't think she's particularly happy to see us.'"

Something was *very* unhappy to see us. It hit on the second-floor landing. I backed against the wall and pushed, unconsciously hoping to get away from whatever was tearing at my nervous system, trying to make myself as small a target as possible. My husband, who was listening to the broadcast said, in his usual understated engineer way that, "you did not sound happy."

I edged off the landing and we went into the front bedroom, considered to be a very "active" part of the Homestead. Years before, I had seen a Victorian death-bed scene there on my first visit to the Homestead.

The room was furnished with a locally-made bed and dresser set. A portrait of Julia Johnston Patterson, wearing half-mourning and a white, ruched widow's cap, like Queen Victoria, oversaw the room. Kim told me, "That's when you really started looking terrible to me! You got real white and seemed to have a hard time breathing. You really wanted out of that room! I felt that there was something that didn't want us to be there."

In spite of his jokes, Sean didn't like it either. "I felt that if anything was going down, it was going to happen there. Something about the way the shadows projected on the walls weirded me out. There was quite a bit of uneasiness in that room. I felt that if I looked out of the windows, I'd see somebody looking in at me. I was pretty damned intimidated by it!"

I couldn't stop pacing. Back and forth, back and forth. I focused on the obsessive, swirling pattern of the rug, trying to outrun whatever invisible energies were stalking me. It didn't feel personal, although I seemed to be getting the brunt of it. It felt like a wave of fury against all of us. "How dare you!" "What incredible nerve!" "Get out!" were the impressions I was getting. Sean and Goatboy had gotten the reaction they wanted, all right. They had stirred up trouble in a big way with their taunts. The ghosts of Patterson were refined, family ghosts, not the sort to respond to vulgarity.

Exhausted, I trudged up the stairs to the third floor where the ghost of a young man in military uniform had been seen during a Christmas candlelight tour (*Haunted Ohio*, p. 88). Just beyond the stairs, the pressure eased up. "Ah," I said, "This is *much* better."

I spoke too soon. There was a small door leading to a servant's bedroom, set aslant under the eaves. Something came *through* the closed door. My daughter saw it at the same instant I did. "There was a man standing right outside the door, blocking the way into that room," she recalled later. "He was older. He wasn't threatening, but he wasn't peaceful either."

Kim told me that our heads swiveled in unison as we stared at the door. Both of us watched as something like a small tornado—a whirlwind of energy—moved slowly into the middle of the group. Unconsciously we fell back as it passed into the center of the group and dissipated.

Door to third-floor attic bedroom

Kim remembers:

Sean was interviewing you, when suddenly you and your daughter looked at the same time to the far corner. There was nothing there. I said, "Do you see something?" You said to your daughter. "What do you see?" She said, "I see a man crouching in the corner." You shook your head, agreeing with her. I said, "Chris, is he happy to see us?" "I think he's frightened and confused." "Well, then maybe we should go." I was watching your eyes and your daughter's eyes as you were watching this man. And through your eyes, I could see what he was doing. At one point, he started to move closer to us. Both of you leaned back a little. I've always trusted you, but this was amazing to me. It was so coordinated, there was no way you could have planned anything like it. The minute you moved back, I started down the stairs. I said, "I'm ready to go!"

I was ready to go, too. The only other oddity of the day was a mysterious odor of tobacco smoke in the downstairs hall, which several of us smelled. I took my daughter to school, went home, and collapsed in bed. I didn't go back for over two years.

On a more recent sunny May afternoon, Patterson Curator Kerry Adams seemed a lot more relaxed when I came by to take some photos. "I think they like me," he said, speaking of the Patterson Homestead ghosts. "Or perhaps it was just a matter of them getting used to me. We've been doing a little more investigation of the family and how they lived here—a little more interpretive focus. And I think the house 'speaks' more, or perhaps we're more in tune with what the house wants to be. It almost feels like they're saying, 'Very good! We'll behave now.'

"Seven years ago I would have said it was baloney," Kerry admitted. But a stint at a haunted historical farm site in Michigan, where ghostly children who died of consumption in the house, still ran and played upstairs, made him more accepting of the unseen.

Kerry has begun to make some beautiful changes at the Homestead. I found the dining room, formerly a rather cold, museum-like room, dramatically lightened, both in physical light and psychic "atmosphere." We stepped into the hall where we had smelled the cigar smoke during the Z-93 radio broadcast. Kerry pointed out a mahogany veneer tall-case clock at the end of the hall.

"This clock was originally in the parlor. We moved it there, under the steps and tried to get it to work. We leveled it, cleaned it. It refused to work. So we moved it over here, at the end of the hall, leveled it out and it works like a charm!"

Kerry has been making an effort to place genuine Patterson family heirlooms in each room. The elegant Federal-style parlor has been painted dark green and now contains the Patterson family Bible. A highly Sabbatarian black horsehair sofa sits in the parlor thinking dark thoughts about the side chairs' frivolous scarlet upholstery. Across the hall is a room that may have served as Colonel Robert Patterson's office. His ledger used to lie open on the desk; along with a quill pen. A former curator told me how she would put the pen in its rack and close the ledger each night, only to come in the next morning to find the ledger open with the pen lying across it. Tiring of this little game, she left the ledger open and the pen off the rack. The playful spirit would then close the ledger and replace the pen on its stand.

A little sheepishly, Kerry told me about his challenge to the Patterson ghosts:

"I had heard the story of how the quill pen would be found in different places. I got to thinking, 'I'm going to move that quill and see if anything happens.' Now this was all done in my head, I didn't tell anybody what I was trying. There were two inkwells on the desk: a glass one and a wooden traveling one with a screw-on top. I took the quill out of the glass inkwell and put it on the desk. A day or two later, nothing had happened. I was disappointed. Three days later, the quill was still there but the wooden inkwell's top had been unscrewed and was lying on the desk with the accession number showing, something we never do when displaying an artifact. I thought, 'Never mind! You fooled me!' And I put the lid back on the wooden inkwell, the quill back in the glass inkwell, and *left* them there. *Somebody* let me know that they are still here."

Another incident Kerry cannot explain occurred in the second-floor room devoted to the twentieth-century Pattersons. There is a case of *objects d'art* collected by Jefferson Patterson in his thirty-six years as a diplomat, and photos and portraits of the Patterson family. Here is Julia Shaw Patterson Carnell, the grandest of *grande dames*, who founded the Dayton Art Institute; Frank Patterson; John H. Patterson, founder of NCR, painted with his son Frederick and his daughter Dorothy. Over the fireplace hangs a sentimental, pastel-colored photo of the Patterson children with their mother, Katherine Beck, who died tragically young. A photo of Frank Stuart Patterson, who died in a test flight at Wright Field, looks out from its frame, eerily like Charles Lindbergh. There is also an intricate Patterson family tree, a handsome brass NCR cash register gleaming like a holy relic in its showcase, and on the mantelpiece, a small bronze portrait bust of John Patterson.

Bust of John H. Patterson with portraits
of his wife and children

"This room carries out the theme of 'NCR and the twentieth-century story of the family,'" Kerry remarked. "And this is something I can't explain. We never had a cash register in the house before. A day or two after the cash register was placed on display, I found Patterson's bust, which I had set straight on the mantelpiece, turned to face the cash register. I asked the summer intern, Jen, the only other person with access to the room, 'Did you touch anything in the Patterson room? Did you dust or anything?'"

"I didn't touch a thing," she told him, eyeing the bust warily. "But it has moved! It has!"

Patterson Homestead feels pleasantly isolated, as if it stood in the middle of a country estate, not on a busy street near the University of Dayton. The property's many trees give it a pastoral air; you almost expect to see sheep grazing on the front lawn.

Many of the other Patterson family homes have been torn down; but the Homestead remains. Perhaps generations of Patterson ghosts have returned here, gathering for a phantom family reunion. It is a happy thought—the older generation watching the children play among the trees, while life flows on around the Homestead, as changeable and changeless as the Great Miami River.

Visiting the site

A meeting room added in 1955 is available for rental by the general public. Patterson Homestead hosts a Christmas Open House and other special events. NOTE: The third floor is not open to the public. Only the first floor is handicapped accessible.

Just around the corner, at 118 Woodland Ave, Dayton, OH 45409-2854, you'll find Woodland Cemetery & Arboretum, a treasure-casket of fascinating monuments and Dayton's dead and famous. It's also the haunt of the Ghostly Girl of Woodland Cemetery (*Haunted Ohio,* p. 67 and *Haunted Ohio IV,* p. 97), and, perhaps, of the ghostly Johnny Morehouse and his equally spectral dog (*Haunted Ohio IV,* p. 98). For an earthly treat, dine at The Pine Club, 1926 Brown St., (937) 228-7463, where even a sitting Vice President of the United States can't make a reservation. There's also a Ben & Jerry's Ice Cream across Brown Street to revive your spirits. You'll also enjoy the restaurants of the Oregon district (East Fifth Street in Dayton), Hickory Bar-B-Que, 1082 Brown St., Dayton, OH 45409-2813, (937) 228-5252, and the raise-the-dead garlic salad dressing at Dominic's, 1066 S. Main St., Dayton, OH 45409-2715, (937) 222-3667.

Directions

The Patterson Homestead Museum
1815 Brown Street
Dayton, OH 45409
(937) 222-9724

I-75 to 35 East to Main Street exit. Take Main St. south, turn left on Stewart St., then right on Brown St., follow to 1815 Brown St.

9

SPOOKS AT SPITZER
Spitzer House Bed & Breakfast
Medina

I ironed my blouse for the evening's event at the haunted Hinkley Library and went out to give my talk. When I returned...I took a hot shower in the deep, old-fashioned tub...I climbed out of the shower, wrapped myself in a towel, and opened the bathroom door to let out the steam. A young woman was standing there.

She was a short, stout woman, in her twenties, perhaps, wearing what could have been a striped skirt and waist or what the Edwardians called a "wrapper" or housedress. She also wore a long apron tied around her thick waist. I could tell her smooth hair was parted in the middle, but I wasn't getting much facial detail other than a heavy jaw.

"Are you pregnant?" she asked me in a curiously nasal tone. Without thinking, I replied, "No, just fat."

"How old are you? Do you have any children? What are you doing here?" The questions came in rapid fire, without waiting for my replies. I stammered answers, more than a little dazed by this chattering apparition. Studying her, I realized she was what might have been called "simple" or "not quite right." ...She was very nosy and completely unself-conscious. Then, just as suddenly, apparently losing interest, she was gone.

From *Haunted Ohio IV*, pp. 123-4

Spitzer House was built in 1890 by a team of builders for General Ceilan Milo Spitzer, born in Batavia, New York in 1849. His family moved to Medina in 1851. Known as "the Genius of the family," the bold, confident Spitzer and his cousin Adelbert were the successful owners of Spitzer & Company, the first company west of New York City to engage in the buying and selling of bonds. Always a gambling man, Spitzer once played Adelbert a hand of poker to decide how to divide up some properties they jointly owned. In 1894, Spitzer married Lilian Cortez McDowell. In January, 1900, Spitzer was appointed Quartermaster General of Ohio by Governor George K. Nash, with the rank of Brigadier General, hence his title. Ceilan and Lilian only lived in the house for about two years before they turned it over to Ceilan's stepmother and father. His half-

Spitzer House Bed & Breakfast

brother Sidney held the lease, which was next taken over by Ceilan's niece, Evalyn. The Spitzers had no children of their own, but delighted in their nieces and nephews. Lilian died on June 18, 1917. Spitzer followed her on February 18, 1919.

The house remained in the Spitzer family for seventy years. Eventually it was bought by Janet and Dale Rogers. "We purchased The Spitzer House as a family home in 1990." Janet said. "I'll never forget when our realtor first took us through this old Victorian. The porch was falling down, plaster was coming off the walls, and the outside of the house hadn't seen a coat of paint in years, and those were the highlights!" But the energetic Janet had a vision and Spitzer House Bed & Breakfast opened in the fall of 1994. Painted a warm peachy-beige, the elaborately gabled house is in the Queen Anne style. It boasts beveled glass entry doors, two cherry staircases, stained glass windows, and a Victorian rose garden.

HAUNT HISTORY

I spent the memorable night mentioned at the beginning of the chapter in 1996. I went back to Spitzer House in March 2000, this time with my daughter.

The carved cherry woodwork in the hall gleamed in the light that filtered through the pink-flowered windows on the landing. It was late afternoon and the parlor's red-glass windows cast a lurid glow on the oriental rugs. A black dress, topped by a large black velvet hat, trimmed with a wisp of widow's veil, was poised on a dressmaker's form by the front window. I whimsically imagined a spatted and top-hatted ghost waltzing the headless dress around the darkened parlor to the ghostly strains of the upright piano.

I reported in *Haunted Ohio IV* that the piano in the parlor played a few notes by itself while I was there. Apparently the song goes on. Janet related a story about a recent performance: "One morning in November at the breakfast table," Janet said, "one of my guests was talking about how they had seen Spitzer House on the Channel 3 news, on a special they had on 'Spirits.' The next thing we knew, the piano played about five notes. We *have* had our ghosts play a few notes for guests in the past but never at the breakfast table for everybody to hear! My guests instantly said, 'There's your ghost!' and then ran into the parlor but there was no one there." The lid to the piano was shut, the way it is always kept, Janet added.

Mice in the mechanism? Kitten on the keys? Or a childlike ghost who just likes to finger the keys at random?

In the entrance hall, Janet pointed out the tinted photo of Lilian McDowell Cortez Spitzer. A descendent of William Penn, she married Ceilan in 1884. The photo shows a formidable-looking lady with a bosom like the prow of a battleship, a fur slung ruthlessly around her neck. She is made of stern stuff, I thought to myself. I wondered what she would make of the forest of cookie jars thronging every square inch of shelf space in the dining room or the pink, heart-shaped Jacuzzi for two in the Honeymoon Suite.

It was in the same entrance hall that a friend of mine had an interesting olfactory experience in January 2000. Nick Reiter and Lori Schillig of The Avalon Foundation [see Appendix 2] were making an investigative visit to the house. Nick wrote:

> I was standing in the wide doorway that connects the parlor with the foyer. The aroma of the house is strong and flowery but pleasant from the many scented candles that Janet and her husband use. Suddenly, for a fraction of a second at most, a very strong scent swept over me and then vanished. I was, and am, hard pressed to define it. I would say that it

seemed to be some very obscure scent of woman's perfume…
The short-lived "olfactory" impression of perfume from times
gone by was quite vivid. Could this have been a residual
energetic pattern…or did a ghost, complete with Victorian scent
walk by me that afternoon?[1]

Upstairs, the spotless guestrooms were draped with lace curtains, net tablecloths, lacy Victorian underclothes, and all manner of
old-fashioned frippery. Each room is named after a person from the
home's history: "Anna's Room," "Ceilan's Room," "Sidney's Room,"
"Evalyn's Room," and has a charming antique button framed on the
door. We went into Anna's Room, where I had the experience noted
at the beginning of this chapter. Leaving my daughter in the room, I
went out in the hall, and chatted with Janet on the landing. I
watched my daughter cautiously approach the bathroom. She
stopped and made a face, just outside it, on the spot where the
young woman's ghost had appeared to me. She looked over at us.
"There's something here," she said, wrinkling her nose.

"That's where the simple young woman was," I told her, briefly
retelling the story. Her mouth fell open. "I read that story you
wrote," she said, "I just didn't know that this was the house!"

"'Anna's Room' used to be my daughter Cheyenne's bedroom,"
Janet said. "She heard strange noises: footsteps, laughter, and talking

"Anna's Room"

in the room. She also heard her name called when she was alone and was often tapped on the shoulder."

A guest had an identical unsettling experience in Anna's Room. She was wakened from a sound sleep by someone who tapped her left shoulder. She woke up and looked at her husband but he was sleeping soundly. She lay back down. Someone tapped her again. She started to ask her husband what was wrong but he was still sleeping. She went back to sleep and got tapped *again*. Despite the invisible interruptions, the sleeper must have had strong nerves because she has continued to be a regular visitor at Spitzer House!

I declined to stay in Ceilan's Room when I first visited, especially after the room lights went out suddenly. Janet's other adult daughter, Misty, didn't find it comfortable either. On a visit by Misty and her husband, she was shaken awake when someone, or something, picked up the end of the mattress and bounced it up and down about twelve inches, enough to pull the covers out. She woke her husband up but he told her she was dreaming. She was too afraid to even go into the hall to check for pranksters so she spent the rest of the night lying awake and vigilant. Now they both refuse to sleep in the room when they visit.

My daughter and I both felt vaguely uncomfortable in Sidney's Room, named for Ceilan's half-brother. There wasn't any good reason—it was as chock full of delightful lace, dolls, and antique china as the other rooms but it had a darkness hanging over it that had nothing to do with the physical world. I knew, but my daughter did not, that Avalon Investigators Nick and Lori had identified that room as the most active in the house. They described it as having a "cold, creepy feel to it," although they were unable to find any magnetic anomalies or capture anything on audiotape or film. Janet told us, "Sometimes my dolls in Sidney's room get moved around, their faces turned or positioned differently, or their blankets rewrapped."

These are Spitzer House's minor mysteries: taps and piano notes and vague feelings of unease. But Janet was thoroughly shaken by what happened in January 2000. On January 24th she saw her first ghost in the house and she isn't sure she liked it.

"I never thought I'd see anybody," she told me. "Can people like you visiting stir things up?"

I made a face. People have often told me that their ghosts became more active after my visit. It has made me wonder if I was poking them with some kind of psychic stick, stirring them up. This time it wasn't my fault. Janet saw her ghost just the day after Nick and Lori visited the house.

"I was so scared, I couldn't move!" Janet said. She had gone into the basement to do some laundry, when there he—or a very strange-looking she—was, standing facing the wall right in front of the slab the drier sits on. "He was very tall, a very wide person. He was the width of the side of the washer. I thought it was a real person who had broken in and would turn around and hurt me."

There was nothing wispy or transparent about the ghost. It was solid, blocking out the washer. The figure was wearing something long and grey—a long grey coat or perhaps a dress. While the body was solid, the face and head lacked definition.

"I couldn't tell if it was a girl or a guy from the hair. There wasn't enough detail. As soon as I could move, I ran up the stairs and locked the door to the basement!"

She stood there for what seemed an eternity. Just then, her husband came home. "Hon! There's someone in the basement!"

Bravely, her husband searched. Not only was nobody there, no windows were unlocked and there were no footprints in the snow by any of the windows.

Having searched, Janet's husband looked at her and said, "I think you saw your ghost."

"I was so scared, I cried," said Janet. "I didn't expect it. It stopped me dead in my tracks. I thought it was a real person. Never once did I think it was a ghost."

Although apparently real, Janet's ghost was unsettlingly ambiguous in appearance. Was it the big, round-faced General Ceilan? Or could it have been the formidable Lilian? It certainly was not the plump, childlike ghost I encountered that October night in 1996.

One more spirit seems to have been added to the Spitzer House guest list: a ghostly cat. While my daughter and I were sitting in Janet's dining room, I kept seeing a cat dart by. Finally I asked, "Do you have cats?" I hadn't remembered any cats from my last visit.

"I used to have a cat. It was my daughter's. But we couldn't keep it because we found too many of our guests were allergic," Janet said. She gave the elderly cat to a friend and it is now dead.

But the cat came back. "About two weeks ago [June 2000]," Janet wrote me, "I saw my cat ghost! I was in the kitchen hugging my husband. I looked down and there was a large, dark brown cat, its ears pricked up, with big gold eyes. It was just sitting there with its two paws in front of it, at attention, very alert. I looked at my husband and said, 'Look at the cat.' then it was gone! It was crazy! Then a couple days later, I remembered you saying you saw a cat."

Jenny, who worked at Spitzer House while Janet and Dale were on vacation, also saw the cat.

"I was in the kitchen, writing down a reservation when I saw something out of corner of my eye. There was a dark-colored cat by the coffee pot. I didn't think anything of it. I have two cats at home, myself. I turned back to the table and when I looked back a split second later, it was gone. Then I thought, 'They don't have cats.'"

A ghost so solid it was taken for an intruder; a phantom feline thought to be a living cat. As Janet said, "That's one thing about the ghosts here, you always start out believing they are real!"

Visiting the site

If you're an antique buff, there are numerous antique shops and malls in the area including the Medina Antique Mall, just east of I-71 on Rt. 18. Akron, Cleveland, and the Cuyahoga Valley National Recreation Area are all within easy driving range. The beautifully restored historic house, Stan Hywet, 714 N. Portage Path, Akron, OH 44303, (330) 836-5533, is open to the public but the staff does not admit to having any ghosts.

Directions

Spitzer House Bed & Breakfast
504 West Liberty Street
Medina, OH 44256
(330) 725-7289

Web site: www.spitzerhouse.com

From I-71, take Rt. 18 West through Medina Square. Continue West on Rt. 18 (West Liberty) four blocks. Spitzer House is located on the corner of Prospect and West Liberty Street.

10

THE FABRIC OF TIME
Stitches in Time Vintage Clothing
Plymouth

Coffins stood round like open presses,
That showed the dead in their last dresses…

-Robert Burns, "Tam o' Shanter" (1790)-

The current brick building was built in 1871. Owner Shirley Wolf showed me a photo of the building when it was an establishment purveying "Gent's Furnishings" and "Clothing." The photo shows two stick-like mannequins standing at attention under the striped awning and a sign advertising "Men's Overalls." Running in front of the building is a wooden boardwalk, like something out of an old Western movie. Copperplate graffiti on the basement stairwell harkens back to the 1880s when the building was M. Shield & Son and Spear & Shields, Men's Clothier and Furnishings. Shirley has another photo dated 1910 when the building housed a bar, billiard hall, and restaurant.

Shirley and her husband Jim have owned the building since 1991. They spent two years restoring it and opened their showroom in 1993.

HAUNT HISTORY

Shirley Wolf has an uncannily nineteenth-century face. When she takes off her modern glasses, with her rosebud mouth and cheekbones of another era, she could have stepped straight out of a tintype. She also has an uncanny feel for exquisite vintage clothing. Painted a muted mauve, her store, Stitches in Time, is a model of what vintage clothing stores should be: clean, well-lit and beautifully arranged with elegant displays. "Marguerite," a mannequin in motoring costume holding a steering wheel, pilots a rocking chair by the door. An old-fashioned bed is piled high with lacy embroidered pillows. Glass cases are filled with the muted shimmer of

Stitches In Time Vintage Clothing

silver, satin, porcelain and rhinestones. Another mannequin is dressed in a rust-velvet bustle dress, so heavy it must have been like wearing sofa upholstery. A silk shirtwaist in the colors of a Monet garden glitters with sequin trim.

"I always liked playing 'dress-up,'" Shirley said when I asked how she'd gotten into the vintage clothing business. "I still do!"

Shirley turned on all the lights and sent me on the prowl around the store. Although there was a creepy spot at the front of the basement and a startling moment with a shelf of mannequin heads, the basement and first floor were fine. It wasn't until I had climbed past the red brocade curtains to the second floor that I felt a shiver.

Among the hats and the furs, I caught the merest flicker of a ghostly lady. I walked around a corner and found myself facing a long hall flanked by a rack of shoes and a neat pile of hatboxes. In the hall I began to notice someone behind me. It was a man. I wondered what in the world a man was doing here. It would be more logical, I thought, to find a lady ghost, but it was no use. It was definitely a male.

He was behind me. I kept getting the words "man-maid." Perhaps it was a phrase he had been taunted with. He was an effeminate young fellow, speaking in a shrill, affected voice. The silly thing is, I can't remember what he said, only the high-pitched voice.

"You wouldn't have dared talk like that when you were alive," I thought. "You're just putting it on for me!"

He glided along behind me as I inspected the four storage rooms carefully crammed with an overwhelming collection of velvets, satins, and laces. Every piece seemed unique, museum quality. Here was a coffee-colored cut-velvet cape trimmed

The haunted hallway

with carnival glass beads and the furry chenille fringe I call "tarantula legs." There was a young girl's bustle dress in white cotton, trimmed in blue ribbons, like a Renoir portrait. An ecru satin and lace 1920s wedding gown competed with a plush cape trimmed with spiky monkey-fur.

The hall ran into a room with high windows overlooking the street. It was filled with shoeboxes, hatboxes, and jewelry boxes, most neatly labeled. It was here that I got a look at the ghost. He was tall and thin and had sandy hair. I wasn't getting much facial detail, except what seemed to be a rather long, pointed chin. I also got the words "haberdasher's assistant."

Back downstairs I thought it best to warn Shirley before we started that I might not be at the peak of my psychic form. After all, I had failed to spot the ghostly Mr. Wilkinson at the Mansfield Memorial Museum the previous day. So my heart sank as she stated neutrally. "You saw a man...."

She kept me in suspense as she described her early days in the new showroom. One dress form with a very heavy base kept moving.

"I swear to you," she said to her daughter Melanie. "each time I look that dress form has moved."

"Are you just now noticing?" said her daughter.

"You know," said Shirley, studying the dress form's costume. "I don't think she likes her bonnet."

"After I changed the bonnet, the form stopped moving.

"There is one place in the store that I am extremely uncomfortable—it's upstairs—the junction between the front room and the first storage room just before it, what I call my "Collection Room" because it mostly has my own pieces in it. When I work up there alone, I have heard footsteps coming down the hall

"I'll say, 'Jim?' Nobody. And I'm constantly seeing a figure going into that room—like a shadow seen out of the corner of my eye. There's just an uncomfortable feeling of being watched. Sometimes I say, 'Take off! Leave me alone!'"

The ghost seems inquisitive and even impertinent.

"I was sitting on the stairway and somebody came down the stairs behind me and was blowing on the back of my neck. I turned and said, 'Stop it!' It's a drafty place sometimes but all the windows were shut. It made me crinkle up my shoulders and neck!"

It was Shirley's granddaughter, Kayleigh, then aged three, who first really saw the ghosts. Shirley emphasized that at the time Kayleigh had not had any exposure to TV or movies. The proud grandma showed me a photo of the little girl dressed in a miniature 1870s outfit with a tiny hoop and muff.

"My daughter was at the store with my granddaughter. Kayleigh ran and hid behind her mother. 'Kayleigh, don't! Move!' said Melanie. The little girl wouldn't budge. 'Somebody's there!' she kept saying. And she kept looking around her mother as if at some intruder.

"About a week later, I was sitting at the sewing machine when Kayleigh crowded between the sewing machine and the desk.

'Somebody's here!' she said.

'Where?' I asked

'There.' the child pointed towards the refrigerator.

"When I looked the wrong place, she said, 'Not there—*there*.'

"Show Grandma."

The little girl took Shirley by the hand and walked her over to the microwave. 'There's a lady. See her?'

"No. But tell me about the lady."

'Her's pretty. She has on a white dress and a beautiful hat. See her?'

"No, I don't, but I think *you* do." Shirley said.

"I felt like she really was seeing something and I really believed her. I was a little skeptical at first, but there was so much sincerity, it was obviously not contrived."

A week or two after that, right after Christmas, Kayleigh was playing in the store by the Victorian sofa when she suddenly ran to the bathroom and shut the door.

"Do you need to go potty?" Shirley asked.

"No."

"Then what did you close the bathroom for?"

"*Him* keeps bothering me and I shut him in the bathroom and him wouldn't stay."

"Oh," said Shirley.

On the same day, the little girl suddenly gathered up all her toys and ran beside the bed and sat down.

"Him won't leave me alone!"

Shirley played along. "Tell him to go away."

Shirley heard Kayleigh say, "GO *AWAY*." She was standing, looking up at someone tall, flapping her hands. "Go away! Go AWAY!"

"Who are you talking to?"

"That man."

"Tell Grandma about that man."

"Him's big." Big, in Kayleigh's world, always meant tall. "Him has a 'stache and beard like Daddy. (who at that time wore a neatly trimmed goatee.)

"Where is he now?"

"She looked at the ceiling. 'Him's gone way up.'

"And I found myself looking at the ceiling too."

"Come with me," said Kayleigh, leading her grandmother upstairs.

"We went to the first room. 'Nope,' said Kayleigh. We went to the second room. 'Nope,' she repeated.

"When we got to the front room, she said, '*There* him is! See him!?' And Kayleigh reached down to pet something.

"'What are you petting, Kayleigh?' I asked her, thinking she was touching an imaginary cat or puppy.

"'Him has a pet chicken. It's soft, white and fluffy!'

The ghosts seemed to have a life of their own. On another day Kayleigh saw the phantom man and the woman fighting. Once she said that the lady was in a closet, looking at the clothes. When Shirley was helping a wedding party try on gowns Kayleigh said, "Him is peeking through the curtains. Him likes to peek!" Still another time, she said that the man was very sad because his little brother had gotten run over and killed.

"I didn't think to ask if it was a wagon or a car!" Shirley said. "That would have solved where this guy comes from!"

If the man was an imaginary playmate, he was a very vivid one. After her initial fear, Kayleigh made friends with the stranger.

"Kayleigh would fall to the floor and say, 'Him's tickling me. Him plays with me. I'm like their little girl.'" It was obvious she could see a man and woman but she mostly talked about the man.

When the child was going away for a few days she told Shirley, "I have to tell him goodbye. Him will miss me." Shirley watched as the little girl hugged the empty air with a blissful smile on her face.

One time Melanie was upstairs helping Shirley sort items to take to a show when she heard an awful noise, a kind of groaning moan.

"What the hell...?" she said.

"Him's looking at your hats," said Kayleigh.

Shirley jumped in, speaking to the ghost. "That's all right, we'll bring your hat back!"

Occasionally Shirley gets a reaction from a customer like the one who asked, "Do you believe in ghosts?"

"Do you?" Shirley asked cautiously.

"Oh yes, in fact, there's a man standing behind you. Whenever there are ghosts around, my hands start sweating." She showed Shirley her palms. They were wringing wet.

"What does he look like?"

"He's tall, with reddish hair, a beard and mustache."

"Answer me one question, Is he malicious?"

"Mischievous, but not harmful." The customer said she wasn't frightened, but she did appear tense. She had expected to spend the afternoon looking at lovely clothes, not running into a ghost.

Another time, Shirley was helping a wedding party from Michigan. She was about to take one woman upstairs when the woman asked her sister, "You coming?"

"No," said the woman shortly.

"Oh come on…"

"I'm NOT and you know why!" said her sister.

"Is there a problem?" Shirley asked.

"There is a man on those stairs and I will NOT go by him!"

On yet another occasion, a customer who told Shirley that the temperature drops for her when ghosts are around got overpowering goosbumps in the Collection Room.

Resuming our tour, Shirley took me back upstairs to her Collection Room.

"I'm not afraid up here. I'm just uncomfortable," she said. We quickly forgot about ghosts in the rainbow of colors and textures as we plunged into Shirley's private vintage clothing collection. She showed me a prize piece: a hand-woven paisley shawl made into a mantle with elaborate multicolor fringe and a French label. It was a masterpiece! As a former vintage clothing dealer, I was thrilled by her personal collection and, like most fabric nuts, I was going "ooh!" and "ah!" and "You paid *how* much?!"

Then Shirley pulled out a midnight blue velvet caplet spangled with silver beads and sequins and trimmed with clouds of fluffy ivory astrakhan. It was like a blaze of stars in a night sky. I went into raptures: "Oh, my God! That is *so* incredible!"

Suddenly I heard the ghost from the doorway. My mouth fell open. He was echoing everything we said!

"He's *mocking* us, imitating our voices," I said indignantly. "He's making *fun* of us!"

"Stop it!" Shirley told him with mock severity.

He grinned. And stopped it.

Back downstairs, I was about ready to go when Shirley asked me, "Do you ever *feel* things?" For a minute I went blank—wasn't that what I had spent the last hour doing? Then I realized that she meant psychometry, the ability to hold an object and draw impressions from it psychically.

Display of children's clothing at
Stitches in Time

"Not really," I said. "Not officially. I can try though."

I thought she was heading for her office to pick up something. I figured it would be something small, perhaps a piece of jewelry. I followed her and we chatted about this and that. She came out of her office again and began to rummage among the children's clothes. I wasn't paying too much attention until she suddenly thrust a baby's white gown at me.

"Here. What do you get from this?"

I caught a glimpse of minute white-on-white embroidery wreathing the neck. It was a perfectly ordinary white cotton gown. I'd seen hundreds like it. But I recoiled in horror. I didn't want to touch it.

"The baby died in that dress!" I blurted, the blood draining out of my face. I was seeing a post-mortem photograph[*] of a baby.

Shirley says I backed away at least six to eight feet, although I have no memory of it. She also says I seemed horrified and distressed and begged her to please put it back.

Then my conscious mind took over and I began to back-pedal and rationalize.

Nobody would sell a dress a baby died in. If the baby *was* dressed in the gown for a post-mortem photograph, they would have *buried* the child in it. It *couldn't* have been a dress for a dead baby....

[*] It was a mid- to late-Victorian custom to take photographs of dead loved ones as a memorial. These were called post-mortems.

"Or the baby was sickly…" I finished weakly. "But I'm seeing a post-mortem."

Shirley smiled a kind of twisted smile and turned the garment's tag around so I could read it.

"Given to me by lady in one of our apartments whose baby died. The gown was purchased by me from the MacIntire estate here in Plymouth. They owned several rental properties in town as well as the dry good store for many years which he had inherited from his father."

I went deathly cold. "I'm scaring myself," I said.

"When I know the history, I write it on the tag," Shirley said, putting the dress back in the armoire, much to my relief.

We chatted a little more about Kayleigh. "She's now seven and doesn't talk about it much. She never called them ghosts. They were always 'ghost people' or 'them people' or 'him' or 'her.'" As if Kayleigh was part of whatever dimension they inhabit.

While Shirley herself was very pleasant and her store was a thousand square-foot fashion plate, I left Plymouth in a thoroughly unsettled mood. The affected red-haired "gent" upstairs I could handle, I could even find him amusing. But the dead baby's gown, with its vision of tiny crumpled hands and stiff, blue-veined eyelids, was too much to bear. I thought of the lovely things I had seen, the clothing for celebration and rejoicing. And I reflected on the common thread of our mortality that runs through the fabric of time, a thread of life spun long for some and for others cut heartbreakingly short.

Visiting the site

The first floor is fully accessible. See p. 12 for more area information.

Directions

Stitches in Time
6 E Main St, Plymouth, OH 44865
(419) 687-2061

Web site: www.stitchesintime.com

Plymouth is at the intersection of Rt. 61 and 603, about 20 miles NW of Mansfield.

11

THREE EERIE PIECES
Punderson Manor House, Newbury
Central Ohio Fire Museum, Columbus
Brownella Cottage, Galion

Ghosts come in all sizes. Sometimes I only collect a fraction of the ectoplasm needed to make a full-fledged ghost story. In this chapter, I present three spectral snippets.

Punderson Manor House

Punderson Manor House, whose story was told more fully in *Haunted Ohio* (p. 24) overlooks a sparkling blue lake, the largest and deepest "kettle lake"** in Ohio. While the lake and park are named for Lemuel Punder, Newbury Township's first permanent settler (1808), the Tudor-style manor house was begun by Karl Long in 1929. His timing couldn't have been worse. He lost his fortune in

Punderson Manor House

**formed when a chunk of partially-buried glacial ice melted

the Crash of 1929 and some say he hung himself from a tree by the unfinished Manor House.

The story is only the first of a number of legends that shroud the Manor House. Did it really serve as an orphanage where a group of children burned to death? Did a teenaged girl drown in the lake? Is the Manor House truly haunted?

My daughter and I visited Punderson on a bright and chilly March morning in 2000. The long, winding entrance road built up suspense, like the opening of Hitchcock's *Rebecca*, when the heroine and her mysterious Maxim drive to Maxim's fabled house Manderley. But nothing could have looked less sinister. The picturesque roof slates, mossy and uneven, the golf cart parked by the service gate, the crackling fire in the reception desk area, the cheery dining room overlooking the lake.

The dining room, with its huge fireplace, was the site of a horrifying apparition of a hanging man, seen by three employees in 1979. Today, the Punderson manifestations seem more prosaic. The servers told me that individual lights blink on and off, although this is physically impossible because the lights are all on one circuit. Sometimes the bar TV will turn on by itself, or, more unsettlingly, the servers will hear it playing, while they can see it sitting there with its screen dark.

Guests have complained of noisy parties going on in the room next door, when they are the only guests in the house. One clerk, thinking that the noise might have come from a clock radio, checked the unoccupied next-door room, only to find the radio unplugged. Other guests have heard riotous music and noise in the room above them, when there *is* no room above them.

I experienced something of this spatial disorientation when I visited. My daughter and I walked up a hall towards a dead end, reached by a flight of stairs. A projecting wall element hid what lay beyond. A ghostly man in a red-plaid shirt came out of nowhere and walked around the projection into what I assumed was another hall. My daughter did not see the man. When we came up the stairs to the "Scenic Room," just past the projection, I was startled to see a blank wall.

The ghost of the drowned teenaged girl is another Punderson legend. Or is it?

A young lady wrote to me, "A few years ago at the YMCA Day Camp, we went swimming in Lake Punderson. I was with my friends. We were seeing who could hold their breath the longest. That's when we heard sharp, high-pitched screams for help. When Stacy came up she asked us if we heard the screams. We all nodded. We all swore that we didn't do it, so we thought it was just some little kid.

"Everybody forgot the whole thing. But just last month I was reading an autographed copy of *Haunted Ohio II*, when I saw something about Lake Punderson. When I finished the second paragraph, those screams echoed through my mind. I realized I had heard the teenaged girl screaming. I never did believe in ghosts until I found out those screams were from a ghost."

There never was an orphanage on the site of the Manor House although some children died in a 1940s fire at a tavern across the lake. Yet I had to step around a ghostly child on the stairs when I visited and a former ranger told me a truly chilling story. There was a fire in an outbuilding whose walls were made of cement block. After the fire was extinguished and the ashes had cooled, the ranger was making the rounds, checking on damage. In the middle of one wall, which had been completely blackened by the smoke, he found a small white handprint, as if some doomed child had crouched there, hand on the wall, while the inferno raged. Just one more Punderson legend?

Punderson Manor House Lodge
11755 Kinsman Road, Newbury, Ohio 44065-9684
(440) 564-9144
Web site: http://www.dnr.state.oh.us/odnr/parks/directory/punderson.htm

Central Ohio Fire Museum

From 1908 to 1981, when it was retired from active service, Engine House Number 16 served the people of Columbus. In 1990 the exterior was restored to its utilitarian brick beauty, with a medieval-style bell tower and the words, "No. 16 Engine House" picked out in raised red brick against the ochre brick trim. Inside you'll find fire engines of many eras, including the heart of the exhibit: an 1881 Amoskeag steamer, a huge engine glittering with polished brass and

Central Ohio Fire Museum

nickel-plate. It could pump 1,100 gallons per minute, the same capacity as today's engines. There is also an 1885 fire bell, as well as helmets, harness, and all manner of fire-fighting gear. The décor leans heavily to shining brass, weathered leather, and, of course, fire-engine red. Like coals that smolder beneath the ashes, some energy continues to haunt the firehouse, just waiting its chance to burst into life again.

"Captain D" was the first captain assigned to Engine House Number 16 just after it was built. He had a reputation for thoroughness bordering on obsession. He'd walk the second-floor locker rooms, checking equipment, then checking it again.

In the mid-1970s a seasoned Chief and a rookie firefighter were sitting in the TV room of the building. They heard a creaking upstairs.

"That's just Captain D," the Chief said casually. "I first heard him when *I* was a rookie." The younger man thought he was joking, but he was dead serious. "No, I've heard him walking all over the second floor. And sometimes you can hear the fire horse noises too"

Others have heard the ghostly footsteps of Captain D roaming the Fire House, pacing back and forth, checking equipment over and over, to be ready for an alarm that will never come again.

Engine House Number 16 was also home to ten fire horses. At the alarm bell, the horse stall doors opened automatically and the well-trained horses moved underneath their suspended harness, which was then dropped onto their backs and quickly fastened to the steamer. A crack team could be on its way in two to three minutes. Harnessed three abreast, they galloped down the streets of Columbus, in a desperate race against the flames.

In 1919, Bill, Rex, and Jim, three distinguished member of the Columbus Fire Department retired. They were the last fire horses in Columbus. But although they have long since gone to that great pasture in the sky, something of their dedicated spirit remains at the Fire Museum. Firefighters have reported hearing the creaking of harness, the snorting of restless animals, the sound of hooves pawing restlessly against the floor, the clang of horseshoe against metal-sheathed doors.

They await the last alarm, those spirited horses. Death has not dowsed their desire to make just one more run, their hooves striking sparks from the ghostly cobblestones.

NOTE: The Museum will not open until 2001. You can call the number below for an appointment or more information.

Central Ohio Fire Museum
260 N. Fourth St., Columbus, OH 43215
(614) 464-4099

Brownella Cottage

Brownella Cottage (*Haunted Ohio*, p. 128) was the home of "The Red Bishop," Bishop William Montgomery Brown who was excommunicated by the Episcopalian Church for his Socialistic and heretical views. The house stood sealed up for over thirty years as the courts wrangled over his will. It is now run by the Galion Historical Society and open to the public. It is believed to be haunted by Mrs. Ella Brown, the Bishop's wife, who died in the

Brownella Cottage

tower room in 1935 and by the Bishop himself, who has been seen in his study and in the glassed-in walkway between the main house and his study.

In June 2000 I took my friend Alexis* to Brownella directly from Oak Hill Cottage (See p. 92). She was already rattled because ghostly places make her ill at ease. As we admired the house, Alexis commented on the beauty of the trees. "I'll bet the Bishop planted them himself," she said. The words were just out of her mouth when we heard a sharp ripping crack above us. A large grey object came hurtling out of the tree, plummeting into the lily bed by the fence.

I walked cautiously over to the spot. Embedded in the lilies was a huge log that had torn off the tree just as Alexis had spoken. It was a weathered grey, with no bark and had obviously been dead a long time. One end was so pointed that I thought stupidly, 'How did that fence post fall out of the tree?' I raised up one end of the log so Alexis could see it. She shook her head.

"I am *never* going *any*where with you again!" she said.

Brownella Cottage

132 South Union, Galion, OH 44833

(419) 468-9338 or (419) 468-1861

12

THE SPIRIT OF THE HOUSE
Oak Hill Cottage
Mansfield

A great brick house, conceived in the most bizarre union of Georgian and Gothic styles...The roof carried a half-dozen high pitched gables; the windows were tall and pointed in the manner of a church rectory, and the chimneys, built of white stone, were carved in the most ornate Gothic fashion.

-Louis Bromfield, *The Green Bay Tree* (1924)-

The exuberant Oak Hill Cottage, considered to be one of the most perfect carpenter Gothic houses in the United States, was built in 1847 for the sedately named John Robinson. He and his wife lived there for fifteen years, raising five children.

Robinson worked for the Sandusky-Mansfield-Newark Railroad, absorbed in 1861 by the B&O. No one is quite sure what went wrong, but in 1861 the Robinsons moved out and the building went back to the bank. It was sold several times, but never actually occupied by the buyers. Perhaps the location was inconvenient—it stood out in the country—or the elegant house was too expensive to keep up.

In 1864, Frances Ida Jones, the wife of Dr. Johannes Aten Jones, fell in love with the house and persuaded her husband to buy it. The furnishings currently on display in the house belonged to the Jones family, who occupied Oak Hill for 101 years. The Jones raised four daughters in the house, losing a fifth daughter in infancy. The girls had the best of advantages growing up: they traveled the world, went to the finest finishing schools, and married well.

Author Louis Bromfield played at Oak Hill Cottage as a child. His grandmother and Mrs. Jones were sisters. Bromfield wrote about the house in his 1924 novel *The Green Bay Tree*, calling it "Shane's Castle."

Dr. Jones was a consulting eye-ear-nose-and-throat specialist and an early distributor of Peruna patent medicine. Although well-to-do, and visited by rich and famous people, there was no question

Oak Hill Cottage

of keeping up with the Joneses. Somehow the Jones family just didn't quite fit into Mansfield society. They were notoriously proud people. There was the usual gossip, as there always is when a man is a cut above and lets people know it. Dr. Jones died in December 3, 1895. Mrs. Jones died of heart disease on December 12th, 1912.

"12-12-12," the curator told me. "And if I found out that it was at 12:12, that would just be too much. ..." (I checked her death certificate. The time of death is stated as 12:15. Too close for comfort...)

The last of the Jones daughters, Leile Barrett, died in 1966.

In 1965, the house and property was titled to the Richland County Commissioners, a move which made the building eligible for historic preservation grants. The Richland County Historical Society owns the contents and manages the site. The enormous carriage house across the street still awaits restoration. Remarkably, most of the furnishings are original to the house.

The scrupulous attention to detail in Oak Hill's restoration is nothing short of incredible. Even the carpets were custom-woven, using as a portion of the original pattern. Astonishing photos in some of the rooms show the décor and the furniture. They could have been taken yesterday instead of in 1896. The house boasts seven gables, five double chimneys and seven marble fireplaces. The Historical Society decorates this already lavish house even more lavishly for Christmas.

HAUNT HISTORY

It was love at first sight. I even drove around the block several times, completely enchanted from every angle. Oak Hill Cottage was the house of my dreams—if only I could shrink it and carry it home to my dollhouse room! It looked like an illustration from *Woodward's Country Houses* or a Currier & Ives lithograph.

The curator unlocked the house for my own private tour. I prowled about the house, moving as quietly as I could. There was something very feminine about Oak Hill Cottage that made me want to speak softly, move soundlessly. If houses can have personalities, Oak Hill Cottage was ladylike and utterly charming.

I padded through the dining room, its windows mullioned in a chevron pattern with cobalt blue glass insertions. A stern black buffet carved with bouquets of dead ducks and a deer's head, dominated the end of the room, an altar to conspicuous consumption. Underfoot, the floor was inlaid with an elaborate knot pattern. Off the dining room, I saw a ghostly woman writing a ghostly letter at the window in the butler's pantry.

Adjoining the dining room was a little sitting room and an amazingly modern bathroom with a copper tub and the earliest flush toilet in Mansfield. Beyond it lay Dr. Jones's office, with his massive desk and bookcases and his leather satchel of remedies. Across the hall lay a breathtakingly elegant reception room running nearly the full length of the house, divided by elaborate pillars. You can almost picture the grand soirees held here, the ladies' jewels sparkling in the flare of the gaslights, the men's stern black broadcloth, the gleam of the little gilt chairs where young ladies gaze shyly over their fans at the young men.

I circled back to the dining room. The back stairs led from the dining up to the maids' rooms and onto the landing where a small door was cut out of the paneling, more the size of a cupboard than a full door. Opened, it revealed a set of very steep, very high steps. A little confused by this arrangement, I crawled up them on my hands and knees, and found myself face to face with a sinister little baby carriage, all rusty black fabric and spidery fringes, topped with a wobbly black parasol like a miniature hearse. It gave me quite a turn, as did the dead baby picture hanging above the child's bed.

It was here that I saw a little boy ghost. He seemed to be about four years old, wearing baggy white stockings and a little suit with scalloped edges on the knee pants, the jacket sleeves and bottom. The curator later told me that one of the Robinson's sons had died in that room. It seemed a cold and inhospitable place, compared to the rest of the house. I imagined what it would have been like to lie in bed, watching that little door, waiting for it to open to who knows what creature of nightmares?

By contrast, it must have been delightful for the children of the house to play on the landing at the front of the house by the Gothic-arched door, under the stained glass window, its colors forming an ever-shifting kaleidoscope on the floor. Perhaps Louis Bromfield played there.

On the second-floor landing and in the child's room, stood glass-front cabinets filled with artifacts of the Jones' lives and travels. Elaborately feathered hats, a still-glossy hank of brown hair, beaded pincushions, moon-faced Japanese dolls, cases of glass eyes, goggling grotesquely up at the viewer. On the wall are framed photos and newspaper clippings showing three generations—Frances Ida's daughter, granddaughter and great-granddaughter—wearing the same wedding gown. The gown itself stands in a case like a glass coffin in an adjoining bedroom. Once white, it has now mellowed to a delicate beige, its beading cascading in a sparkling torrent down the laced bodice and skirt.

From the second floor, I descended to the blandly modern basement, all cement block and pale, shiny paint. One edge of the large meeting room was curtained off. Gingerly I peeked behind the curtains where cleaning supplies and other items were stored. Near the furnace area, I ran into a truly curmudgeonly ghost: a very grumpy old man who didn't want me there at all! Later when I told the curator about it, she immediately called up her brother, who had helped stoke the furnace at the house when he was a boy. Without knowing what I had just said about the basement, he described being terrified when he went over in the afternoons to shovel coal into the furnace.

"I felt like somebody was watching me and didn't approve of my being there." 'I'm just putting the coal in,' he'd tell the invisible watcher. 'I'm not doing anything wrong.' And he wouldn't linger...

All through the house, I got the feeling that someone was watching me, shyly, from behind doors, and around corners, someone who just didn't want to show herself. Downstairs in the entrance hall, I sat down in the docent's chair and closed my eyes. The feeling that someone was standing behind me was so strong, I opened them again and looked cautiously behind me. As I gazed up at the elaborate metal and glass chandelier in the hall, several of the bulbs suddenly went out. I stood up to leave and walked down the hall towards the exit.

Something made me stop and look back at the front door. The bulbs on opposite sides of the chandelier suddenly began to blink alternately off and on, rhythmically, like Christmas lights. On, off, on, off. I smiled. It seemed a clever and amusing thing for the ghost to do. Then the blinking stopped and all the bulbs came back on. I walked back to where the chandelier was burning and jiggled the bulbs to see if they were loose. They weren't, although the curator later told me that the right bulb does frequently go out and come back on by itself.

Suddenly I realized that there was a lady standing at the top of the stairs. The light was behind her so I could only see her in silhouette. She wore form-fitting 1880s clothing. She was so happy and so welcoming that it brought a smile to my face. I felt she must have been the perfect hostess.

"How do you like my house?" she asked me in a silvery voice. Then she was gone.

The curator is convinced that I saw Mrs. Jones. Mrs. Jones was very proud of the house. Known as "Frank," a common nickname for girls named Frances, Mrs. Jones was a perfectionist when it came

The blinking chandelier in Oak Hill's hall

to her house and its upkeep. The perfect house, the perfect hostess, the perfect afterlife?

On a subsequent visit, I brought along my friend Alexis*, who is very sensitive to "atmosphere." She knew nothing of anything I had seen or experienced and had never heard of the house.

"The first thing I sensed was an overwhelming pride. These were very, very proud people. And the lady of the house was unusually 'house-proud.' But there was something about the portraits of Dr. Jones," she said uneasily. "There was something cruel about his eyes, like someone who had seen too much."

Indeed, the portraits of Dr. Jones show a rakish, bright-eyed, sharp cheek-boned face, the face of a soldier or adventurer, not at all the sedate visage of a highly respected otolaryngologist.

Had Bromfield seen the portrait of Dr. Jones at Oak Hill Cottage when he was young? For this is how he describes the fictional master of "Shane's Castle:"

"It was a lean face, swarthy and flushed with too much drinking, the lips red and sensual, yet somehow firm and cruel. The eyes, which followed you about the room were large and deeply set and of a strange deep blue like cobalt glass with the sun shining through it. It was the portrait of a gentleman, of a duellist, of a sensitive man, of a creature haunted by a temper verging upon insanity…The portrait whose handsome, malignant eyes appeared to follow them with a wicked delight."

To *my* wicked delight, one of the lights of the hall chandelier went out as Alexis stood under it. I whooped and she jumped, not knowing what the fuss was about. Alas, it was just the bulb that usually goes out. The opposite bulb did not blink.

The curator is constantly shepherding busloads of people through the historic building. She told us that "On a couple of different occasions, people would be in the house, only get as far as the parlor and say, 'There's something here. I can't stay.'"

I could have stayed all day, and all night. In fact, I would have stayed forever, happily haunting Oak Hill Cottage for the privilege of living in such exquisite surroundings. One can see Mrs. Jones drifting through the rooms, straightening a cushion here, flicking a speck of dust from a mirror there, touching a ghostly hand to an arrangement of flowers. The light falls through the jeweled windows, just as it did in her day. The chandeliers glitter, just as they did in her day. Chances are, Mrs. Jones would find herself very much at home here. Chances are, she does.

Visiting the site

See p. 12 for more information.

The curator recommends The Flying Turtle at the old Mansfield Airport for good sandwiches, 501 Airport Rd, Mansfield, OH 44903-8993, (419) 524-2404. Also try Brunches Restaurant, 103 N. Main Street, (419) 526-2233 and Coney Island Inn, 20 S. Park St., (419) 525-1506.

Directions

Oak Hill Cottage
310 Springmill St.
Mansfield, OH 44902
(419) 524-1765

I-71 to Rt. 30 to Rt. 13, which is N. Main Street. South to Surrey Rd. to Oak Hill Cottage. The Cottage stands between N. Mulberry, Springmill Street and Oak Hill Place, on a hill and it is the most distinctive building in its neighborhood. From downtown Mansfield take Park Avenue West to Bowman St. to East 6th St. to Mulberry St. North to Oak Hill Cottage. From the West, take Rt. 30 to Rt. 39, which turns into Springmill Street.

13

MY OTHERWORLD AND WELCOME TO IT
Thurber House
Columbus

Columbus is a town in which almost anything is likely to happen, and in which almost everything has.

-James Thurber-

It looks like an ordinary brick house from the turn of the nineteenth century with a touch of stylish Eastlake trim. It is a typical, middle-class house, full of Mission oak furniture, dark paint, beveled glass and respectable lace curtains. But it is the house where the bed fell, where there were nightly alarms and diversions, the house where the electricity leaked out of the sockets if you didn't screw in a light bulb. And, of course, the house where The Ghost Got In one night. It is The Thurber House, home to a man of extraordinary comic vision: writer and cartoonist James Thurber.

Listed on the National Register of Historic Places, 77 Jefferson Avenue stands on a quiet street that loops around a central green space. A delicate statue of the Unicorn in the Garden, one of Thurber's most charming and cynical stories, stands on a shrub-shadowed mound on the green across the street. The house displays Thurber memorabilia—first editions, original drawings and manuscripts. It is now a gallery and writers' center hosting frequent author readings, children's programs, workshops and classes. A writer-in-residence inhabits the attic, often the only *living* soul on the premises.

HAUNT HISTORY

The night of James Thurber's own uncanny encounter was November 17, 1915, exactly forty-seven years after the Ohio Lunatic Asylum, which stood on the site of the Jefferson Avenue house, burned down, killing seven people.

Here's what "Jamie," as the Thurber House associates like to call him said happened:

My own experience in this mysterious area came one night…in a house my family lived in at 77 Jefferson Avenue in Columbus. It consists of the heavy steps of a man walking for nearly a minute around our dining room table, while I was in the bathroom upstairs drying my face with a towel before going to bed. At the time I was a junior in college, studying journalism, and a non-believer in ghosts. In fact, the word ghost never crossed my mind that night. I thought a burglar or a crazy man had got into the house. My father

Thurber House

and younger brother were in Indianapolis and I knew that neither of them would walk silently around that table. I roused my older brother from sleep and brought him to the head of the back stairs that went down into the dining room. As soon as he reached my side, the steps ceased. Finally, in something like terror, he asked me. "What's the matter with you?"

I said, in a loud voice, "There's someone down there," and up the stairs right at us, two at a time, came the heavy steps of a running man. Without a word, my brother ran into his bedroom and locked the door. I stood there until one more step would have taken the invisible thing into me and then, by a reflex I slammed the door at the head of the steps.[1]

Thurber turned this real and terrifying experience into a hilarious short story, "The Night the Ghost Got In," in which Thurber's grandfather shoots a policeman, and comic mayhem ensues. In real life, he took the incident very seriously and investigated, discovering that a man, despondent over an unfaithful wife, had shot himself in a second-floor bedroom, after pacing around the dining room table.

In *Haunted Ohio*, (p. 157), I told of Thurber's factual recounting of his family's ghost story, as well as some subsequent tales of the ghost. I concluded, that "the old specter" continued to walk, or rather run, long after the Thurber family moved away. He still does.

Thurber House holds a series of Literary Picnics each year: lawnside dinners and readings by various authors with an Ohio connection. In 1992, one of these authors spent the night in Jamie's room on the second floor. At 3 a.m., she heard footsteps come up the stairs, then the door burst open, to reveal—nothing. She knew no one was in that part of the building except her. The current writer-in-residence, living on the third floor with his family, swore that he and his family had not left their quarters that night.[2]

While making repairs in the writer-in-residence apartment on the third floor, the maintenance contractor closed a closet door. When he walked past the door later, it was again open. He closed it, a little puzzled, and returned to his work. The next time he walked through the room, the closet door was ajar. He *knew* he had closed it, so he shut the door, then tried to reopen it, to see if the latch was defective. The door simply would not open. It even acted like it was locked—except that there was no lock on the door. After several unsuccessful attempt, the man said, "I'm out of here until the ghost quiets down!"[3]

Two weeks later, the new writer-in-residence moved into the apartment. After unpacking, she came into the administrative office and asked, "What is it with that closet in my apartment? It won't stay closed." Even more chillingly she saw the reflection of a man in a picture hanging on her wall, not once but several times. Her radio also gave her trouble: it would mysteriously turn itself on, tuned to a completely different station and the sound of static. Perhaps the ghost is on some difference frequency, trying to be heard.[4]

Thurber's brother Robert was quite a sports enthusiast. Displayed in his room at the house is a picture of Buckeye football player Chic Harley, who was the idol of OSU during 1916-17 and 1919. When the staff went home for the day, Chic's picture was sitting securely in its usual spot on the mantle in Robert's room. When the staff returned the next morning, the framed picture was still sitting in the same place but the photo's glass was shattered all over the floor. No one had been in the house after the staff left.[5]

In June 1992, the administrative assistant heard the chair roll over the floor in the second-floor office directly overhead, then she heard footsteps cross the floor. No big deal, you might say. Except that she was the only person in the building at the time. For months after this incident, books would often fall off the Thurber Country Bookstore shelves behind her as she walked between the living room and the bookstore. The bookstore, incidentally, is housed in the dining room where Thurber and his brother heard the ghostly footsteps of the doomed man pacing around the dining room table.[6]

A Thurber House Journalist-in-Residence in 1994 wrote a fascinating article about her eerie experiences in the attic apartment. She says,

"I have to start this story the way I always do: by telling you right up front that I do not believe in ghosts. That said, this is a story about how I lived for a summer in the attic of a haunted house... I don't believe in ghosts, but I do believe in inexplicable occurrences, and surely the things that happened to me (and my dog) the summer of 1994 in Columbus, Ohio, can't all be explained away."

She explained how the Thurber House staff members had told her stories of seeing and hearing the ghost.

"These stories were entertaining, but they had a nasty way of coming back to me late at night...

"During the day, the house is busy; phones ring, staff members chat and visitors pop in and out of the rooms, plunking the keys of the typewriter Thurber used at the New Yorker and staring at the photos on the walls. But at 5 p.m., the house empties. The other buildings along the street also close, and after dark Toby and I were the only living souls on the entire block.

"And it was usually after dark when I, too, heard footsteps, treading one floor below....Sooner or later, whoever lived there heard footsteps...

"Every night, when I shut off the lights and crawled into bed, I left on the air-conditioner so I wouldn't have to hear them, but I heard them quite often anyway. At first it was only occasionally, but for a stretch of about two weeks in July I heard them every night, walking briskly up and down the hallway one floor below.

"One night I leashed up the dog and crept with him down the attic stairs to see if we could find the source of the noise. We peeked into the silent bedrooms and the cool white bathroom and then, spooked by nothing more than the darkness, dashed back up the stairs to the apartment, where I had left all the lights burning and the TV blaring, and slammed the door.

"Toward the end of the summer, Toby saw the ghost downstairs.

"It was evening, and the house had been shut up for the night - the shades drawn, the lights turned off, the doors securely locked. This was my favorite time to prowl the museum. As long as some late-afternoon light filtered in from outside, the house seemed friendlier at this quiet time of day.

"I wandered into the museum bookstore, and Toby meandered down the hall. And then, just as before, I heard him growl.

"He was two rooms away, in the museum's front parlor, staring at a velvet couch beneath a leaded-glass window. The evening sun was setting, and the sky outside was a dark pink and gold.

"Just as before, Toby's body was tense. And just as before, he growled, though this time with more certainty.

"I tried to walk past him to see what was alarming him, but Toby wouldn't allow it. He moved in front of me, blocking my way, keeping me from the couch and whatever invisible thing was on it.

Thurber House stairs

"It was a full minute, I think, before he stopped. His snarls trailed into silence, and then he walked hesitantly to the couch and sniffed it all over in puzzlement.

"It was as though whatever had been there had disappeared...

"I haven't come to any great conclusions about what happened in that house that summer. I talk about it pretty freely, but whenever I do I always preface my story with the statement, 'I don't believe in ghosts,' before going on to mention the ways I experienced the ghost. Somehow, that doesn't feel like a contradiction...."

The old specter still walks, even in this new millenium. What is he looking for? Does he still seek his erring wife? Or is he walking away from the certainty of his own death? As long as I can keep walking, he tells himself, I *can't* be dead. Perhaps he is living in his own fantasy world beyond the grave, the secret life of some of postmortem Walter Mitty.

Visiting the site

The second floor is not handicapped accessible. The attic Writers-in-Residence apartment is not open to the public. There is only a limited amount of free and metered parking available on the street.

Other local haunt-spots: The Palace Theatre, 34 W. Broad St., Columbus, OH 43215 (*Haunted Ohio II*, p. 173)

The Clock Restaurant, 161 N. High St, Columbus, OH 43215. The incredible stained-glass façade is worth a visit. (*Haunted Ohio*, p. 171)

Schmidt's Sausage Haus, 240 E. Kossuth St., Columbus, OH 43206 is reputed to be haunted by the original owner. They also serve out-of-this-world fried red cabbage and light-as-ectoplasm cream puffs.

Directions

Thurber House
77 Jefferson Ave.
Columbus, OH 43215
(614) 464-1032

Web site: http://www.thurberhouse.org

Located just one block from the Columbus Museum of Art, 77 Jefferson Avenue is one block west of the I-71 intersection at East Broad Street. Or take I-71 to the Broad Street exit. Go East on Broad Street to Jefferson Avenue. Turn left. Thurber House is easily recognized by the large cement Thurber-esque dogs in the yard.

14

A ROOM WITH A BOO
Old Stone House on the Lake
Marblehead

They fall, and leave their little lives in air.
                              -Alexander Pope-

Old Stone House on the Lake, Marblehead

The Old Stone House was built of local stone in 1861 by Alexander and Almira Clemons, thirty years before the town of Marblehead was founded. Alexander opened the first limestone quarries in the area. Alexander and Almira, whose stone-faced portraits hang in the second-floor hallway of the bed and breakfast, had thirteen children. Each of those children had at least five children and each of *those* children had at least five. In the end, it was impossible to decide who should inherit the house unless they each carted off a wagonload of blocks, so the house was sold—a move some family members bitterly resented after three generations of occupancy. It has served as a bed and breakfast for over twenty years. Brenda and Dan Anderson bought the house in 1995.

HAUNT HISTORY

The tall, upright house is built of the local grey stone. Its outer layer is called "shell stone," and bears the marks of waves and tiny shells. The house's knife-sharp edges are softened by the charming landscaping, the golden gazing ball, the weeping trees. It has an austere New England feel about it. As soon as Brenda showed me my room I saw that the original house had not been particularly elegant. The walls were coarsely whitewashed over rough plaster. The room was large and bare.

I must have looked dismayed because Brenda asked me anxiously, "Is the room OK?" The raw-looking plaster melted back into charming candy-pink and mint-green floral wallpaper. The large bare space gave way to a cozy room furnished with antiques and lace curtains.

"Fine, fine," I said hastily, hoping she'd just think I was tired instead of time-warping.

After I returned from dinner, Brenda, her son Troy, and daughter-in-law Stacy came out to the terrace by the water to tell ghost stories.

"What brought you to bed and breakfasting?" I asked Brenda, a vivacious, good-humored woman with a tip-tilted nose and honey-streaked hair.

"Insanity!" she answered instantly, with an infectious laugh. "I was tired of teaching and wanted to do something else. I had no *clue* what I was doing!" And she never dreamed that there would be something extra included with the property.

Brenda noticed that extra something about their new house her first week there.

"I was here by myself. My husband hadn't arrived yet. It was little things—like things being moved around, especially in the kitchen. Whatever it was moved all the cat food! I had all these little cans—about fifteen of them—lined up in the pantry and they were gone. I searched and searched. I went through every shelf in the pantry and I couldn't find them. 'I'm going crazy, I said to myself. 'I *know* I put them in here!' I had to go out to the store and buy more. A few days later, there were all the original little cans, neatly lined up in the same place."

Another curious property of the house was doors that opened by themselves, even when they were shut and locked.

"I'd say to myself, 'Am I not closing the doors right?' I'd find them open, but locked."

Skeptics might say that in an old house with uneven doorframes a gust of wind might easily push open the doors. But these are *interior* doors, never exterior.

"I hear walking upstairs when nobody's there, across the common area on the third floor, then back. The room has the original bare wood floor. It sounds like a child marching quickly back and forth."

"There used to be a painting of a woman hanging in the hall outside Room 2. One day it was storming, so I was running around closing windows and I ended up in the kitchen. I heard this BOOM BOOM BOOM!

"'What the...?!?' I said. I ran upstairs and found the picture lying ten or twelve feet away down the hall. Now this was a *square* picture frame and it's not like it could roll. The same thing happened again about a week later. 'OK, I'm getting rid of it!' I said. *She* didn't want it there and if I can't have things the way I want, *she* can't have things the way *she* wants them!"

"She" is possibly young Tabitha Johnson, daughter of a family who married into the Clemons line. A friend of Brenda's who has done some research on the original Clemons family says that Tabitha was sitting playing in one of the floor-level windows on the third floor [in what is now Room 11], when she fell out of the small window. It is thirty-five feet to the ground, and she died instantly. She must have been small, because the windows are tiny, just a little over two feet high and three feet wide.

"I get pretty freaky and uncomfortable with the whole thing," admitted Brenda's daughter-in-law Stacy, a dark-haired Minnie Driver look-alike with a touch of sunburn.

"She's skittish," agreed Brenda, smiling.

"I kept house here in the summer of 1998, after Brenda broke her leg," Stacy said. "Whenever I would clean the two bathrooms on the third floor, I would shut the doors. And when I came back, the doors would be open again. 'C'mon!' I'd say, 'Leave me alone! I've got to get my work done!'"

Even the bathroom in the Anderson's private living quarters is apparently not off-limits to the ghost.

"Whenever I'm in the shower," Stacy said "I swear there's a shadow moving outside the shower curtain. I'll peek out and there will be nobody there."

"The same thing has happened to me," Stacy's husband Troy said. "The bathroom door sticks. It will *not* blow open. I'll hear the door open and think that somebody has come in to get something out of the medicine chest. Only I don't hear the door open for them to go out. So I pull the shower curtain back and nobody is ever there. Sometimes I'll find the door solidly closed, even though I just heard it open. Or it will be open, vibrating back and forth."

For a long time Troy was skeptical, even though the ghost knew his name.

"My bedroom is at the back of the house on the first floor. I heard a faint whisper calling my name, 'Troy...Troy....' I didn't think anything of it. Until I personally see something, it's just a story."

Troy, a tall, broad-shouldered law student, didn't seem like he would be either afraid of or gullible about the supernatural. But "it" soon became more than a story.

"We had a bunch of family visiting and they were in my room. I was on the living room couch when I woke up suddenly. I've been a volunteer firefighter so I wake up quickly and completely. In the door between the living and the dining room was a white figure. There was no detail: no face, no fingers or anything. It was just a blob and, although it sounds like a cliché to say it, it was hazy around the edges. I sat up quick! It disappeared." He showed me on the door frame how tall the figure had stood. It was a little shorter than my five-foot one-inch height—about the size of a pre-teen girl.

The sighting was an intriguing confirmation of an experience a guest had in Room 2. The guest woke to see an adolescent girl standing in the doorway to her room. The woman described the ghost as a short, pre-teen young lady with dark, bobbed hair and bangs. With more presence of mind than *I* possess, the guest didn't think anything of it. She just rolled over and went back to sleep!

On the same night in Room 5, something called one guest's name a couple of times—actually whispered in her ear—"Winnie! Winnie! Winnie!" Winnie called to her friend, who was sleeping in the same room with her, "Sandy?" Sandy didn't answer. When Winnie finally felt safe, she got up and found Sandy sound asleep.

Room 11 is perhaps the most active room in the house. Brenda calls it "The Three Bears" room, for its nursery décor and its three beds. A previous owner found what looked like the impress of little footprints on the bedspreads. A guest who was sitting on her bed, saw an indent forming on the bed beside her, as if an invisible body had settled down for a chat. Guests often ask about the room, "Did someone die in here?" It has an unsettling energy about it. Brenda says that things also seem to be more active from the end of July to the beginning of August.

I took many photos of Room 11. Reviewing them that night in my room, I noticed twin streaks of light in nearly every photo (see Fig. A), all of them over the farthest window in the room. They looked suspiciously like a reflection rather than a wraith. The next morning, I went back up to Room 11 and removed the pictures from the wall, hid the shiny-covered books from the bedside table and shrouded the last brass bed frame with a towel. I still got streaks. I couldn't figure out what was reflecting! I buzzed back and forth, covering up this book, and changing that picture. I could feel something in the room with me. Finally I removed an enameled metal sign that I had mistaken for a puzzle. It had just enough reflec-tive qualities to

Fig. A: Room 11 streaks

bounce light into the pictures on the wall, which then arced the light onto the ceiling. Bingo. No more light streaks. End of mystery. Or so I thought.

Instead I got orbs. An orb super-imposed on a streak (see Fig. B) in one photo; a plain vanilla orb in another. And still another tiny one bouncing around on the floor of the

Fig. B: Room 11 orb

Commons room. Brenda saw the pictures and smiled.

"That little stinker's just hanging around up there!"

The energy in Room 11 is very strong, playful, and lively. People talk about the natural resilience of children. But I think that if I had fallen out of a window and died on the pavement, it would have put me off playfulness forever.

One previous owner was really afraid of the invisible guest and supposedly even held an exorcism. Brenda suggested that the ghost wasn't fond of the previous tenant either. The woman wasn't the neatest housekeeper in the world and often she would leave the breakfast dishes on the table and the beds unmade in the morning. She would return from her job and find that her clean laundry had been kicked downstairs!

Brenda, on the other hand, is an immaculate housekeeper. She has also added her special touches to the house: hand-made quilts, a banquet of blue and white china plates hung over a bed, a vintage typewriter, the thinly-sliced cinnamon-flavored apples on the morn-ing pancakes—and her own refreshing brand of common sense.

"I'm not afraid of the ghost. I don't pay a lot of attention. She's just a little mischievous. She hasn't ever really hurt anyone or anything. If she takes something and I ask her to, she'll put it back. If I say, 'that doesn't go there, don't move it again!' it works!"

As a former teacher, Brenda knows that you have to be firm with children—even ghostly ones.

Visiting the site

Be sure and see the Marblehead Lighthouse, just a short way up Rt. 163. The turnoff is not very well marked and the road looks like the driveway to St. Mary's Orthodox Church. Richmond Galleries, 417 W. Main St., Lakeside Marblehead, OH 43440-2249, (419) 798-5631, has an incredible collection of lighthouse/maritime theme art. Schoolhouse Gallery, housed in a picturesque old school building at 111 W. Main St., Lakeside Marblehead, OH 43440-2200, (419) 798-8332, is another good collection of shops as is Just for Ewe, 9523 E. Harbor Rd., Lakeside Marblehead, OH 43440-1728, (419) 798-5151. Historic Johnson's Island, site of a

Johnson Island Cemetery

notorious Civil War prison camp, (*Haunted Ohio III,* p.152) can be reached via a causeway off Rt. 163 as it curls around towards Sandusky Bay. There is a small charge for cars.

Directions

Old Stone House On the Lake
133 Clemons St.
Lakeside Marblehead, OH 43440-2265
(419) 798-5922

Rt. 2 to Rt. 163, which goes directly into Marblehead. Turn left on Clemons St. which is almost directly across from the Schoolhouse Gallery. The street dead-ends at the Old Stone House.

15

THE CITY OF THE DEAD
Hopewell Culture National
Historical Park
Chillicothe

Our dead never forget this beautiful earth,
for it is the mother of the red man.

-Attributed to Seattle, Chief of Dwamish, (1854)-

NOTE: The stories/opinions expressed in this story do not repre-
sent the views of the National Park Service.

The Hopewell culture flourished from the Great Lakes to the
Gulf of Mexico between about 200 BC and AD 500. The Hopewell
were known to be hunters, gardeners and gatherers. They built
elaborate series of earthen mounds and enclosures as places of
worship and to honor their dead. They also crafted sophisticated
ceremonial objects using materials like copper from the Great Lakes,
marine shell from the Gulf of Mexico, and mica from the Appala-
chian Mountains. Ohio is unusually rich in Hopewell sites. The
Hopewell Culture National Historical Park in Chillicothe now pre-
serves and interprets Hopewell Native American civilization at five
major mound centers, along with a museum collection at the Mound
City Group. The site was a ceremonial gathering place and a
necropolis where the dead were cremated or buried.

The site was also the home of Camp Sherman, a huge U.S. Army
training camp hastily built during World War I. The soldiers in-
creased the population of Chillicothe from 17,000 to 60,000 in only
three months. When the Army came in to build Camp Sherman,
they casually leveled all of the mounds except one, the so-called
"Death Mask Mound," to the height of around one foot. Recruits
would run up and down the "Death Mask Mound" as a training
exercise. It was said that the Army builders could put up a barracks
in twenty minutes on the leveled mounds. The structures were

Hopewell Culture National Historical Park

flimsy, drafty, and proved the perfect breeding ground for the Spanish Influenza.

In 1918 the Influenza epidemic ripped through Camp Sherman, killing 1,177 soldiers. Not the sick-to-the-stomach flu bug we are used to, the disease was a virulent pneumonia that specialized in the slaughter of the young. Living under crowded conditions, the soldiers were especially vulnerable. Many were boys straight from the farm, suddenly exposed to a million new germs against which they had no defense. At the height of the epidemic, up to 131 men per day died at Camp Sherman. The dead were stacked like cordwood in the nearby Majestic Theatre (*Haunted Ohio IV,* p. 178). They were embalmed on the theatre stage while the undertakers pumped their blood into the alley behind the theatre, still known today as "Blood Alley." It seems horribly ironic that this peaceable place dedicated to the Hopewell dead became a death-trap for so many young soldiers.

The entire camp was torn down in 1920 and 1921. Much of the wood was salvaged and used to build houses in town. The Mound City Group was declared a National Monument in 1923. In 1946 it became part of the National Park Service.

HAUNT HISTORY

When I first called the Park, I spoke to then-superintendent John Neal.

"I've heard you have ghosts," I said.

There was a long silence.

"Oops," I thought, "maybe that wasn't such a good question, right out of the blue."

Then he started to laugh.

"Well, it's very, very difficult to explain. Some of the people who work here would admit there are phenomenon here. We just refer to it as "the Hopewell." Perhaps we're lightheartedly whistling past the cemetery. Certainly things happen here that are difficult to explain.

"Here in the administration building, four people work in a two-story building. Sometimes when people work early or late, they say it sounds like someone is opening the kitchen door and walking into the kitchen. No one is ever there. Many of us have experienced this more than once. We just don't pay much attention anymore. Some people have taken to locking the doors when they're working by themselves.

"Then there are the usual things that are 'misplaced.' And things that happen when we're doing certain kinds of archaeological work. When we're excavating, which happens once or twice a year, it seems like there is a rash of different kinds of failures. The telephone system goes down, water problems, electric problems. They happen in groups. One maintenance man told the archaeologist, 'If you'll let me know when you're excavating I'll be out of the park!'

"These things just seem to happen, just a little more often than coincidence. Nobody has ever been harmed; nothing has been damaged. Nobody has ever seen anything—or if they have, they haven't admitted it! I have seen or felt the results, though. You'll find oddly placed things. You leave something on a shelf, you find it on the floor in the morning. I think it's part of the attraction of the site. We have a regular clientele of people who come hoping to experience something. If they hang around here they will!"

It was a scorchingly hot June day with thunderheads building in a bright blue sky when I visited Chillicothe. I asked Megan and

Angela, Park Guides, about their experiences with the spirits. They also laughed when I mentioned the door opening.

"Oh yes, it opens. It's always the right one, never the left, which most people use to go in and out of. It will open about a foot, very quietly, then close."

They are also uneasy about going into the museum exhibit area at night, feeling like they are being watched.

"It's dead quiet. And so dark in there..." said Megan. "I go in to check the gauges and I say to whoever, 'I'm just checking!'"

Constance Jones, Park Biological Technician, believes that the door opening is just the wind blowing it open. However, she added, "When I'm at the Visitor Center desk alone, I see things out of my peripheral vision. I'll be reading with my head down and will see something pass in front of me, just a shadow."

Jennifer Pederson, the site archaeologist, who helped me with the historical details, smiled as I asked about ghosts. "I haven't seen anything. I'm waiting!" she said wistfully.

I wandered through the darkened exhibits room before going outside. I had seen Hopewell and Adena artifacts as a child at our local museum, mostly dusty scraps of pottery, flints, and a few decorative pipes. Nothing prepared me for the elaborate range of horned headresses, copper turtle shells, twisted copper horns, a mica plaque, an elegant peregrine pipe, and a raven effigy pipe. Pieces seemed to have been ceremonially broken—ritually "killed" to accompany those dead, who were dismembered then burned in special pits. Perhaps the ritual was to keep the dead from coming back; perhaps it was a way to ease their passage to the sky. Or perhaps it just takes less wood to burn body parts.

Outside, the site was beautifully green and lush. A long straight cement track leads to the perimeter mounds. It ends abruptly in a hexagonal pad, like a jumping-off place to sacred ground. An enormous cottonwood tree stands like a sentinel at the entrance. Some have said that the tree is sacred; that you should ask the tree's permission to enter.

In spite of the destruction caused by the Army, the site still represents a stupendous achievement. The mounds aren't simply heaps of dirt. They are elaborately layered constructions of sand, shells, and rammed clay. These earthworks represent several hundred years of concentrated and organized labor by the Hopewell.

I wandered around to the various mounds, reading the plaques. There is the Mound of the Pipes where nearly 200 pipes were excavated, perhaps a tribute to their maker, the man buried there. A series of posts outlined the remains of a charnel house,

Hopewell Death Mask

the building where the dead were dismembered and then cremated. Insects sizzled in the grass. The wind sighed in the trees. I felt suddenly exhausted. I wanted to lie down and sleep on the grassy curve of Mother Earth. There are tales in the British Isles of mounds, places of mystical power, that open up to admit anyone foolish enough to sleep on them to a fantastic and terrifying land. I kept walking.

Roughly in the center of the circle of mounds stands a high and conical shape, the so-called "Death Mask Mound." It is named for a mask excavated in the 1920s that is made from the head and facial bones of a human skull. The skull mask is pierced by a series of holes around the bottom edge, perhaps to attach a drape or dangling ornaments. The photo of the reconstruction of the mask gave me a nasty shock, even in broad daylight. Of all the digital photos I took at Chillicothe, only the photo of the death mask stubbornly refused to load into my computer. The message read something about the "corruption of the file." Finally, inexplicably, it loaded and you can see the gruesome result here.

For me the death mask was the most terrifying thing about the site. But this was only my own modern mind-set. We cannot know what the mask meant to the Hopewell or what emotions it created in the viewer or the wearer. But the park seems a very calm, mystical site now, certainly not a place of evil. It was an important place to the Hopewell, judging from the immense effort put into creating the earthworks. It is a place of spiritual power and should be treated with reverence.

Still, I would not like to be out among the mounds after dark. I would be afraid I would hear the soft hack of flint on bone, the snapping of sinews, the bubbling of marrow. I could not bear to smell the scent of roasting flesh rising with the smoke. Or to see standing in the mists, a figure with the face of a skull, a living man, looking through dead man's eyes.

And what of the doors that open and shut by themselves? Is it the ghost of some Hopewell Medicine Man, intrigued by the novelty of hinged doors instead of deerskins? Or is it some poor dead soldier from Camp Sherman, seeking the gate back to life, each time he opens the door a little more desperately, hoping to find himself back among his living comrades on the other side.

Visiting the site

There is a fee to visit the park. The Visitor Center and most park trails are handicapped accessible.

Other local haunt-spots, Crosskeys Tavern (See p. 129).

See what's playing at the Majestic Theatre, 45 East Second St., Chillicothe, OH 45601-2543, (740) 772-2041 (*Haunted Ohio IV*, p. 178).

Or just drive around town, enjoying the incredible range of old houses and savoring the history of the area. Chillicothe was the first state capital of Ohio. The elaborate Courthouse is a favorite of mine.

Directions

Hopewell Culture National Historical Park
16062 State Route 104
Chillicothe, Ohio 45601-8694
Phone: (740) 774-1125

Web site: http://www.nps.gov/hocu/

The park's Visitor Center is located three miles north of Chillicothe, Ohio on State Route 104. The Mound City unit of the park is located two miles north of the intersection of US 35 and SR 104.

16

LITTLE CAT FEET
The Buxton Inn
Granville

"All right," said the Cat; and this time it vanished quite slowly, beginning with the end of the tail, and ending with the grin, which remained some time after the rest of it had gone.

-Lewis Carroll, *Alice's Adventures in Wonderland*-

In 1812, the state of Ohio was a mere nine years old. But roads were opening up the frontier and those roads carried coaches and wagons. In 1812 Orrin Granger built the original Buxton Inn, then known as "The Tavern." It served as a mail depot and stagecoach stop on the Columbus-Newark route.

Major Horton Buxton owned the Inn from 1865 to 1905. Ethel "Bonnie" Bounell, a singer and actress, ran the Inn from 1934 until her death in 1961. She willed the Inn to her friend Nell Schoeller, who ran the establishment until 1972. For much of that time, Major

The Buxton Inn

Buxton, Miss Schoeller's beloved pet cat, was her companion and Inn mascot.

In 1972, former teacher and principal Orville Orr was writing drug education programs for the State of Ohio. Audrey Orr was a part time kindergarten teacher and full time mother of two daughters, Melanie and Amy. At the urging of Robbins Hunter, a Granville Preservationist, the Orrs approached Nell Schoeller about the possibility of buying the Buxton Inn. Miss Schoeller was impressed with their plans for restoration of Ohio's oldest continuously operated inn in its original building and agreed to sell. After two years of intense restoration, the Inn reopened on Friday the 13th, 1974. The Buxton Inn continues to be a historic getaway and popular spot for weddings and special events.

HAUNT HISTORY

With its salmon-pink clapboard and white fretwork balustrade railings trimmed with graceful 18th century urns, the Buxton Inn has the charm of a miniature Mt. Vernon. Surrounded by tall trees, the Inn looks cozily compact. Inside you'll find ballroom-size dining rooms, an atmospheric Victorian dining parlor, the casual basement Tavern Room where drovers used to eat, sleep and carouse, and also several ghosts. In *Haunted Ohio II*, I told of the ghostly doings of Major Buxton, a dead-ringer for John D. Rockefeller, who still keeps an eye on the Inn. Ethel "Bonnie" Bounell, "The Lady in Blue" is particularly fond of haunting Room 9. Her ghostly gardenia perfume has been scented throughout the Inn. Other ghosts include noisy wagon drivers down in the Tavern Room and Miss Schoeller's cat, Major Buxton.

Mrs. Orr told me that when the Inn's ghost stories first started making the rounds of the newspapers, she and her husband were accused of making things up for publicity. As a result, they made a rule that no staff members are to talk about the ghosts, unless they are asked. So I asked.

I spoke to Sandy James, the Inn's night auditor. When she first applied for the job she was told, "We've never been able to get anybody to stay here at night."

That would have put me right off of applying, but Sandy wanted and got the job. At first she didn't associate a lot of the occurrences with the ghost. She'd smell Bonnie Bounell's gardenia perfume in the hallway and think, "Did I spray some room freshener?"

She would unlock and then try to open the door to the rear serving stairway. It would act like it was nailed shut or like someone was holding it from the other side even though she knew it was unlatched. A little later, she would go back upstairs, lift the latch and the door would fall open.

She also heard voices down in the Tavern Room. One night during the World Series, Sandy heard noises down there. The door was locked so she listened at the door. She thought the bartender had brought in a radio or little TV to keep track of the Series. When the bartender came in the next day he denied he had any such gadget.

"I didn't know any of the ghost stories," Sandy told me. "One day, I copied the Inn stories out of the *Haunted Ohio* books and took them home with me. I started reading my daughter the stories and when I read about voices in the Tavern Room, gardenia perfume, and mysteriously sticking doors, I thought, 'So *that's* what they were!'

"The only place that really bothers me is the Tavern. We always lock the door because the bartenders complained about things being moved and disappearing. Down in the Tavern I feel there is somebody watching me all the time. I won't go down there until somebody else comes onto the desk in the morning.

"In the Fall of 1999, I was at the desk. All but the immediate lobby area was completely dark. I heard somebody walking down the downstairs hall. The footsteps were so heavy, creaky, and loud that I thought somebody really was in the Inn. I actually ducked down behind the counter to hide. 'This is crazy. I am nuts,' I thought, crouching down. The footsteps went away and I finally got up enough nerve to go peek down the hall. I turned on the lights and walked to the back of the building. Everything was OK.

"Now I have a system so I can monitor things. I walk the whole place every single night and test the doors and turn on the same lights in the same order so I can tell if lights have been switched off or doors unlocked. I think I would just pass out if I saw anybody! If I say it nice and loud maybe they'll hear me!"

Julia Pappas was another Inn employee I interviewed. When she first came to the Inn, she said, "I don't believe in those things."

"It doesn't matter," Lora, in housekeeping told her. "It's going to happen anyway!"

Julia was forthright. "I told Lora, 'The first time I see anything, you'll get *pneumonia* from the breeze as I get out of here!'

"I personally have not experienced anything. But I've heard some of the stories from our guests and I've seen pictures. This last New Year's Eve [2000], some revelers took a picture in front of the front door. A few days later they came back and showed us the photo. In the background is a woman who is dressed in what looks like our waitress costume, a calico dress and tiny mob-cap, standing among the group. You can't see a face, just the dress and the hat."

"I *have* experienced the front door opening and closing by itself. I say to myself, 'Well that's the wind.' The printer goes on by itself. I say, 'That's just a power surge.' I keep trying to find excuses not to believe in anything..."

"Lora told me that after they clean a room, they put fresh mint candies on the bedspread, then they lock up and listen at the door. Sometimes they'll hear the TV go on after they lock the door. So they unlock it, go back in, and find the TV on and the mints gone from the bed."

Dotty has worked at the Inn for three years. She also began with, "Now I've never seen anything *personally*. But there are just little things that make me wonder. I don't know that it's ghostly, but I particularly have trouble with doors and keys. Early one morning I was at the front desk. There was a gentleman having breakfast in the dining room. He came out and I heard him messing with the door for a long time. Finally he came to the desk and said, rather embarrassed, 'I can't get out the front door.'

"I tried the door two or three times and I could *not* get it open. So I went back to get Mr. Orr. He followed me to the front door where I took the doorknob and opened it right up!"

A day after this had happened, a guest approached Dotty and said, "You're going to think I'm crazy. I'm staying in the Thrall Room. My key won't let me in."

"I took my other key and we went right in. Later, I tried the original key and there was no problem. It's things like that that make me wonder!

"I've also seen a lot of photos that guests have taken that make me question: Smoky images where you knew there wasn't smoke. I

Buxton Inn Room 9

saw one taken in Room 9. It looked like a smoky haze, but you could definitely make out a hand and a thumb."

Room 9 is one of the more active rooms in the building. It formed part of Ethel "Bonnie" Bounell's living quarters, and she died there in 1961.

Dotty once stayed in Room 9.

"It was July 9, 1997, my ninth wedding anniversary. All night I felt like somebody was playing with my hair around my ear. I said to myself, 'It's just your imagination! You know the history and you're imagining things!' Two years later, I was talking to a guest who asked me if I had had any experiences. I laughed and said, 'No, no experiences, except the time my imagination got the better of me in Room 9.'

The guest took it very seriously. 'Don't you know that's what the cat ghost does, that it plays with the guests' hair?' she said."

This phantom feline is "Major Buxton," a fifteen-pound cat, who served as the Inn's mascot in the 1960s. You can see a charming folk-art portrait of the smiling cat curled on the Buxton Inn's oval sign.

I was speaking at the Grandview Public Library in October 1999 when a lady shared her story.*

"I had read your book [*Haunted Ohio II*] and decided to go stay at the Buxton Inn. I spent the night in the haunted room and it was beautiful! I just loved the whole Inn! The interesting thing was, there was a cat in my room. It kept putting its paws up on the window, which was painted shut, as if it wanted to get out. I said to it, "No, kitty, you can't get out that way." It jumped up on my bed and kneaded the covers with its feet. I enjoyed having it around."

The next morning she went to check out and mentioned how she had enjoyed playing with the cat in her room. The clerk just looked at her. "We don't have any live cats at the Inn," she was told.

Laura Cunningham was one person everyone told me I *had* to speak to. I finally tracked her down by phone and she had a marvelous tale to tell about her encounter with the ghostly cat of the Inn.

I was the only person in the building one morning. I was back in the pantry, setting up the coffee pots, juice tubs, etc. To my left was the back staircase the servers use to access the upstairs dining room. We don't use it very often. It's very narrow and steep. There's one door to that stair, at the top of the stairs and you have to unlock it from the hall upstairs. I hadn't done that yet. I was filling the juice tub, walking back and forth to the refrigerator and the breakfast buffet table. Out of the corner of my eye, I saw something sort of *plunk* down the stairs, like the way a ball bounces. I do have a cat at home and I thought, "That sort of looks familiar...No," I thought "it's just early..." I put it out of my mind. I finished with the juice and turned to pick up the tub. I was facing the stairs. Standing there, plain as day, was the fattest cat you've ever seen, with this deer-caught-in-the-headlights look! It was made out a thick, foggy, translucent substance. You could tell it was a cat, but I could see through it, like looking through frosted glass. I thought, "I don't need this! It's too early! Just go away!" At that the cat disappeared as quickly as it came.

Just two days later, Laura was again working the early shift. She started her day doing some paperwork at the front desk before setting up breakfast.

I was the only person in the building. The Tavern is directly below the desk area. Some of the equipment in the basement makes noises, like the ice machine, but below me, in the Tavern I heard what sounded like things moving and falling, but not breaking. I thought, "I've never heard *that* before!" It was *not* the ice machine. "OK, fine," I thought, "maybe they've got something new downstairs." And I continued with my paperwork.

Next I heard the two upstairs hall doors to the balcony both slam at the same time. I thought, "Those shouldn't be open!" They're kept locked at night and I hadn't unlocked them.

I thought it was odd, but rationalized that maybe the night auditor had unlocked the doors before I got here and the wind just pushed them open.

As soon as I thought that, I heard footsteps in the upstairs hallway at the front of the building.

"Mr. Orr, is that you?" I called upstairs. No response. Typically if he's coming over he'll call.The footsteps paused in the hallway at the edge of stairs. I just stood there and listened. Then I didn't hear anything and I hoped that whatever it was had moved on. I checked the computer to see if anyone was staying in the rooms off the balcony. They were vacant. Then the footsteps moved into the Yellow Room Dining Room directly above me. "OK," I thought, "this is a little odd." I stood there petrified, then I heard the silverware moving around, the glasses clanking, and the footsteps walking all over the dining area. "This has *got* to be Mr. Orr!" I thought. "Why is he moving all the silverware?"

I heard the footsteps leave the Yellow Room and start down towards the front of the building where there are only two doors at the end of the hall. One door goes to the balcony; the other goes to an office and most of the time this door is kept locked. I heard the footsteps go over to the door. I heard the latch click, and the door open and close. "That HAS to be Mr. Orr!" I thought.

This time I was brave. I grabbed a fire poker and went *slowly* upstairs, looking around. I didn't see anything. The Yellow Room looked just as it should, with the tables all set. Then I went over to the office door. It *was* locked. I knocked on it gently. "Mr. Orr, are you there?" I asked. There was no answer. "OK," I said loudly, "I'm going back downstairs now."

I finished my paperwork and didn't hear anything more. "It must have gone away," I thought. I decided to go back and do the breakfast set-up. As I started back the hallway, I could see into the main dining room. And through the doorway, I saw the tail-end of a whitish gown, made of that foggy, translucent stuff, whisking into the pantry doorway. "Oh my gosh, that's weird!" I thought.

I stepped into the dining room. The pantry doorway opened by itself. Normally the door takes a major effort to open because it's on a spring. But this opened and stood open for probably 30 to 60 seconds. And then it fell closed.

I just stood there. Once it fell closed. I walked up to the door and put my ear to it. I didn't hear anything so I pushed the door open and poked my head in. Nothing. So I went into the pantry and started my breakfast routine.

As I started the coffee, I heard the heavy walk-in refrigerator doors open back in the kitchen. The gaskets make a rubbery, sucking noise. The handles make a large click. I ran around the corner and looked back through the kitchen corridor, expecting to see the doors open or just closing. They were all closed.

I yelled out, "Mr. Orr, are you here?" There was no answer. "*Anyone* here?" I called, a little more firmly. No answer. I thought, "Maybe there's some weirdo in here, playing jokes. I've got to check it out." Bravely I went straight to the back of the kitchen. *Every* walk-in was LOCKED.

"Fine," I said. "I'm finished back here." I went back up to the desk and stayed there until another human being came in.

On New Year's Eve 2000, a gentleman and his wife brought in what appeared to be their grandmothers for New Year's Eve. The man had a digital camera. He was taking photos and he went outside to take some of the Inn with all its lights. He came back in and the look on his face was priceless! He kept saying, "I don't believe it!!" as he went through the photos. He showed Melanie [the Orr's daughter].

In the photo, you could see, standing on the sidewalk, what appeared to be a man wearing a top hat with a long full coat and a cane, just standing there, looking out at him. It was really striking because everything was so visible, so plain, except that there were no eyes, nose, or other facial features—just dark spots. All the details are in that sort of foggy stuff. I told him, "You have to keep that. Don't get rid of that. Very rarely do they appear where you can see so much detail."

Mrs. Orr has seen this photo and others like it but, unsurprisingly, none of the photos could be located. It is always the fate of ghostly pictures to disappear.

Mysteriously locking doors, sounds from the Tavern Room, unexpected extras in photographs, footsteps, and a ghostly cat chasing polter-mice: these motifs weave in and out among the tapestry of life at the Buxton Inn. When you visit, take your camera, an extra skeleton key, and perhaps some catnip. And keep an eye out for Major Buxton, padding majestically through the Inn. Cats, alive or dead, always act as though they own the place.

Visiting the site

The Greenhouse and Main Dining Rooms are wheelchair accessible and have first-floor restrooms. There are several first-floor guestrooms. However, all have one or two steps at the entrance.

There is a fascinating local museum, the Granville Life-Style Museum, 121 S Main St, Granville, OH 43023-1408, (740) 587-0373. This Victorian Italianate house built in 1870-71 offers tours and lectures on period clothing and furnishings.

Other local attractions include Dawes Arboretum, 7770 Jacksontown Rd, Newark, OH 43056-9380, (740) 323-2355 and the Robbins Hunter Museum, 221 Broadway E, Granville, OH 43023-1305, (740) 587-0430, an 1842 Greek Revival House. Minutes away is Moundbuilders State Memorial, 99 Cooper Ave, Newark, OH 43055-2422, (740) 344-1920. Kenyon College (*Haunted Ohio*, p. 139) is only thirty miles north at Gambier.

"Major Buxton" as seen on the Buxton Inn sign

Directions

The Buxton Inn
313 E Broadway
Granville, OH 43023
(740) 587-0001

Web site: http://www.buxtoninn.com

From Cincinnati: I-71 N. to 270 Outerbelt. Go east around Columbus to Rt. 70 E. Take 70 E. to Rt. 37. Take 37 N. to Granville. At the traffic light (Broadway) turn right. The Inn is two and one half blocks on the right.

From Cleveland: I-71 S. to Rt. 37 just east of Delaware. Take Rt. 37 E. to Rt. 161. You will go through Sunbury, Johnstown, and Alexandria. At Rt. 37 and 161 turn left and go approximately 4 miles to Granville. Take the second Granville Exit, turn left and go to the traffic light (Broadway). Turn right at Broadway. The Inn is two and one half blocks on the right.

From Dayton: I-70 to Rt. 37 N. (about 20 miles) Take 37 N. nine miles to Granville. At the traffic light in Granville (Broadway) turn right. Buxton Inn is two and one half blocks on the right.

17

TOM, DEATH, AND HARRY
Crosskeys Tavern
Chillicothe

Three ghosts went to a party and they really celebrated.
By midnight, what were they?
Three sheets to the wind!
-Anonymous joke book-

Since many Chillicothe town records were lost in the "Great Fire" of 1856, it is difficult to be precise about the Crosskeys building's history. Given the age of the town, there were probably several buildings on the site before this one. The Crosskeys building may have been built in the 1880s and seems to have been a place of public entertainment for quite some time. Sun's Bar and Grill occupied the building in the 1930s as did Shine's Restaurant, an elegant, dressed-up lunch counter to judge by its 1933 photo. Tom Burke bought it with partners Dale Perry and Pete Van de Carr and made it the Crosskeys in 1973, taking the name from a pioneer-era tavern.

HAUNT HISTORY

It was synchronicity at work: just up the street was Mourning's Office Supply. Directly across the street was the Left Over Shop. For something—or someone—has definitely been left over at the Crosskeys Tavern in Chillicothe.

The day began inauspiciously: my fax machine blew up, I couldn't find my car keys. I nearly called and canceled my appointment with Tom Burke, the owner of the Crosskeys. I was in a frazzled mood by the time I got to Chillicothe. But driving around the rows of beautiful brick Queen Anne houses, beside the dreaming ponds by the YMCA, past the unique courthouse, as elaborate as a Baroque church, I calmed down. I parked and walked up to the Tavern. There I found, to my dismay, that Tom Burke had gone out and wouldn't be back for several hours. I began to wonder if a prankster spirit was bedeviling me!

Making the best of it, I asked barmaid Louann Carl if I could wander around. "Help yourself!" she said cheerfully, pointing out the basement stairs and turning on the light.

The light didn't seem to help much. I looked gloomily down the aged linoleum stairs. A step from the bottom, I caught my toe and pitched forward, catching myself on the wall. The dimly-lit hall stretched away to the right into a black hole. Inexplicably, I began to shake. I ducked into a pantry full of shelves of canned tomatoes and cash register tapes. It felt safe there.

Across the hall was a grimy alcove housing a huge old-fashioned fuse box and low tables covered with junk. The light from the hall seeped into the alcove but as I stood there a sooty darkness spread rapidly over my eyes. When I stepped back into the hall my eyesight returned. Each time I leaned into the alcove the smoky darkness came back. "Perhaps it was a shadow man you walked through," suggested my fellow ghost hunter Nick Reiter later.

Basement hall at the Crosskeys Tavern

I am glad I hadn't heard his suggestion at the time. In the light from the hall I could only see a few feet into the end room—there were dusty, empty shelves, a row of kegs. And I was afraid to go on. There was a warning, unspoken, but unmistakably real. It was not hostile or threatening, but it strongly suggested that I should stay close to the hall. I stood in the doorway and began to shoot photos blindly in the dark, wondering if anything would be revealed as the flash briefly lit up the room. Every few shots I would flee back to the canned goods, feeling like a swimmer coming up for air.

As I looked at them later, the photo results were ambiguous. While there were odd reflections and images, I had no way of knowing what was potentially ghostly and what was natural, caused by some reflective item stored in the blackened room.

Upstairs again, I wandered into the back lounge. A hand-lettered sign on the door read, "Keep door closed. AC on."

It was hotter than Hades. The carpet felt moist underfoot, like moss. Lurid orange-red lights glittered over the rows of glasses like the glow of hell itself. Behind the bar hung devilish horned masks, a nude mermaid figurehead, a vase shaped like a skull. Privately I dubbed it "The Inferno Room." A presence stood back in the shadows, amused and watchful. Then Louann came into the bar and turned on the lights for me. The presence melted away.

Everybody in the bar seemed to know "Harold" as they call him. Gordon Hixon and "Spike" Spears are regulars and have heard many tales from patrons about the resident ghost.

"Tom and I were hauling stuff out of the basement and I felt a blast of cold air. Now there's no windows and no outer entrance in that basement," Gordon told me. "I swear I felt a tap on my shoulder."

"He opens my cooler doors all the time," Louann chimed in. "I feel like he's kind of watching over the place."

"And it's always been a 'he'." Spike said. He shook his head. "You know, Marcia could tell you stories. I wish she was here." The front door opened. "Well, speak of the devil...."

In walked Marcia, coming to pick up her pay envelope. Louann handed it to her. She opened it and stared. It was empty, except for the fifty-one cents that had fallen into her hand.

"Harold's out on a spending spree!" teased Louann. Marcia took the ribbing about the ghost good-naturedly and told me of her own problem with the basement.

"I didn't see anything," said Marcia "but," she added darkly. "I don't go to the basement any more. The only time I was down in the basement, all the lights went out. I've been down there only once in seven years. I don't do basement!"

Louann told of setting up for a banquet in the room upstairs.

"I swear I heard somebody walk upstairs. It spooked me so much I went down and asked if my husband Tim or Scott had come up. Nobody had."

Louann's husband Tim is the kitchen manager. "I've felt the presence," he said. "I'll see a shadow or feel a breeze go by, especially in the basement. I've also heard footsteps in the lounge. The floor creaks under the carpet and you can hear somebody walking."

"Tom's got stories," Louann said. "I wish he was here."

The door opened and in walked Tom.

He made the rounds, glad-handed his customers, poured himself a Coke and sat down to toss off stories about "Harold" in his deep, cigar-flavored voice.

"I first ran into him in December of 1973. Nobody's ever *really* seen him. He's not been as active recently—he's getting old." He paused and re-lit his cigar.

"I shouldn't say that. Every time I say that, he acts up."

It seems natural to refer to Harold as "he." He's as much a fixture of the Crosskeys as any of the regulars. Tom told me how Harold got his name.

"I was sitting in the back room [the lounge] with a friend and co-worker named Bill about two or three in the morning. We were closed and it was real cold outside. I went to the bathroom and when I came back, I felt a blast of cold air.

'You dummy!' Bill said, 'You forgot to close the door.'

'I did not,' I said. And we kind of went back and forth about it.

So I walked over and I found the inner door open and the outer door closed and locked. I closed the door and sat down.

There was another blast of cold air.

'Can't you do anything right?' Bill said.

I got up. It was open, so I closed and locked it again.

There was *another* blast of cold air.

This time Bill closed it.

No sooner had he sat down, than we got hit with another blast of cold air. This time we *both* went out to shut it. It was open again.

'That's a ghost—or something like it,' Bill remarked.

Three weeks later, on a Sunday afternoon, Bill and I were doing some pipe work in the basement, when the lights all went out.

'Goddamn bulb blew,' Bill said. The light switch was still on and the lights were out. We got the bulb changed and the lights came back. Then they went out again. Bill was upset.

'Harold!' he yelled, 'you cut that out!'

The lights came back on and *stayed* back on.

'Why'd you call him Harold?' I asked Bill.

Bill shrugged. 'Seemed like a good idea at the time.'

Tom continued, "It's not malignant, never hurt anybody. It just plays. The usual stuff: noises in the middle of the night, doors open, lights go on and off—sometimes moving the switch, sometimes without. A favorite trick is to catch you in the basement and turn the lights out. This happens so seldom, we don't carry a flashlight. You'll be groping your way halfway up the stairs and then the lights will come back on. He puts us through our paces!

"Things fall off the wall. Usually they don't break but sometimes he screws up. We had a picture in the back lounge, by the beer cooler, leaning up against the wall at an angle. It fell over with nobody near it. It was physically impossible. I just yelled at him, 'You're not supposed to be destructive!'"

Deb worked at the Crosskeys from 1992 to 1999.

"I didn't believe anything they told me about Harold. Nobody does at first. I thought it was a just a story Jim the cook was telling me. Jim warned me that I'd meet up with Harold someday. It was actually a couple of months later in October. We kept a twelve-pack of Coke on the ice machine by the kitchen. A full can came flying out, about two inches from my nose! Now I could understand one rolling out if they had been laying on their sides. But they were upright!

"Jim said, 'Yep, it's Harold. He's just playing games with you.'

"One time I was at the front of the bar, getting ready to open up. I could see Jim in the back. And I felt somebody touch my shoulder! He left his hand there for a couple of seconds like he was holding me! I think he liked me after that...."

"Sometimes we'd hear the water go on in the kitchen for no reason. One Halloween, Harold threw a wine glass clear across the room. It didn't just slide out of its holder—it *flew!* We think maybe he was mad because we were talking about him."

Deb had heard that back in 1930s the front of the building was the Sun Tavern while the back was Club 19, owned by a shady character named Tom. He was into gambling and he got killed in the back alley. "That's who they think Harold is."

Through the years, Deb mentioned Harold's antics to various beer distributors. One of them was intrigued.

"Where does he live?" he asked.

"Probably in the basement," Deb answered.

So the distributor hid his business card in the basement, wedging it up on top of the rafters where no one could see it. Deb was the only person to know about the business card. Three months later the distributor found the card gone. Deb said she didn't think anything of it because "Harold's just Harold!"

Only one person has ever gotten a glimpse of Harold.

"The Health Department lady was doing an inspection in the basement when she came running upstairs. 'Tom, there's a man down there!'" She had seen a man standing in the shadows of the back room where I had hesitated to go. "We just assumed that she saw Harold/Tom or whatever.

"Sometimes you'll be sitting in the lounge and you'll feel this weird cool draft. We say, 'Harold's walking through.'"

It's almost like he owns the place.

Is it possible that ghosts take on the character of the places they haunt? If so, Harold is a hail-fellow-well-met, a regular. He's a low-key prankster spirit, like that tiresome friend from high school who still plays practical jokes. Not knowing the history of the building makes it difficult to find out "Harold's" identity. We don't know where he comes from, what century it is for him, except that in whatever twilight place he inhabits, it is never closing time.

Crosskeys Tavern

Visiting the site

See p. 118 for more local haunt-spots.

Directions

Crosskeys Tavern
19 E Main St
Chillicothe, OH 45601-2504
(740) 774-4157

Take Rt. 35 to the Rt. 50 exit. Go west on 50, which is Main Street.

Grays Armory tower

18

ESPRIT DE CORPS
Grays Armory
Cleveland

This gray spirit yearning in desire

-Alfred, Lord Tennyson-

In the nineteenth century, every major city had its own militia company of men aged eighteen to sixty-five. They were all volunteers and they had their own uniforms, weapons, flags, bands, and traditions. The Cleveland Grays uniform was based on the 1837 West Point Cadet uniform, a gray jacket trimmed with gold and black braid. Their motto was *Semper Paratus*: "Always Prepared."

In 1861 the Grays were the first Cleveland group to leave for the Civil War. While their initial enlistment was for ninety days, when it was up, the Grays came home and re-enlisted as individuals. The Grays fought at First Manassas and at Phillipi, where they captured a Confederate cannon, now displayed at the Armory. Between the end of the Civil War and the turn of the nineteenth century, the Grays kept themselves in readiness, training with other state Militia, holding a two-week encampment at Chagrin Falls every summer and preparing for the building of a monumental armory building.

In May of 1893, the Cleveland Grays laid the three-and-one-half-ton cornerstone for this modern-day castle just south of the historic Erie Street Cemetery, the oldest burial place in the city. The huge blocks of rough-hewn sandstone, window grates designed like rows of spears, and a five-story tower were designed to emphasize the power and majesty of the militia.

In subsequent military actions, the Grays fought in the Spanish-American War. They rode with General Pershing in the campaign against Pancho Villa and they fought in the Great War, associated with the 145th Infantry.

However, in 1917, military authorities in Washington decreed that private militias weren't prepared enough to serve as regular battlefield soldiers. Despite their gallant record, the militias were seen as local volunteers rather than professional soldiers. The government decided to found a standing national army with the National Defense Act of 1916. Members of militias were told that they could either become members of the National Guard, the Reserve, or disaffiliate. The Grays, notwithstanding their distinguished history of service, chose to stand down, becoming an educational and social nonprofit association.

The original drill hall at the back of the Armory burned down in 1921. Initially, local newspapers wrote that the fire had been set by communist invaders; investigation revealed a more prosaic electrical malfunction.

Just as the European castle was the military and social center of a community, the Grays Armory hosted many brilliant social events. This was the site of the first concert of the Cleveland Orchestra and the first performance of the New York Metropolitan Opera in Cleveland. The first auto show in Cleveland was held here, as was the first Home and Garden Show. John Philip Sousa brought his band to play at the Armory. Presidents Roosevelt, McKinley, and possibly Taft shot pool here. Today the Armory is open for a variety of private, civic, and political functions.

HAUNT HISTORY

The huge sandstone blocks were a rough, soot-stained brown, scarred by time and weather. The top-heavy tower, its battlements alarmingly overhanging its base, seemed a grizzled veteran of many sieges. The massive building looked like it should sink into the ground under its own weight.

My daughter and I found Mr. Frank Tesch, the Armory Administrator, in his office in the base of the tower. I noted an original tiled fireplace, the framed medals and decorations, and portraits of Generals Pershing, Marshall, Eisenhower, and Westmoreland. The name plate on the desk read, "Major General Frank Tesch."

"We have 175 members. Five do all the work," Mr. Tesch said with a smile. He was a man of the World War II generation with an easy-going manner. But beneath his folksy charm, you could sense a dignified man of high personal standards and hard-won experience of the world.

He took us on a tour of the ground floor. A heavy wooden staircase led upwards to the left. The scarlet banner of the 112th Regular Engineers was framed on the landing wall. Something—perhaps a man—was standing on the landing looking at us but I didn't get more than a glimpse. The entrance to the enormous ballroom still had its original sliding pocket doors and the brass rings for the heavy curtains that hung there to keep out the drafts from the main door. Although the roof of the Ballroom/Drill Hall has been replaced since the fire in 1921, something of the flavor of an old-fashioned political rally hall remains in the vast expanse of floor, the hanging balconies and the banners. You can practically hear the cheers, see the bunting.

The Ballroom boasted a Wurlitzer Theatre Organ brought from a theatre in Pennsylvania and restored by the Western Reserve Theatre Organ Society. Mr. Tesch showed us the shrouded organ console and noted that organ concerts are given at the Armory three times a year. Some of the thirty-two-foot pipes loomed against the far wall.

"There's 10,000 square feet of ballroom," Mr. Tesch told us, detailing some of the notable events held there. And while he went away to answer the phone, gunfire echoed beneath our feet, making me jump.

"I hope they have a shooting range in the basement," I said to my daughter nervously. "Otherwise, I'm having a *really* vivid flashback."

Returning from his call, Mr. Tesch confirmed that the local police use the shooting range downstairs. With the history of the Grays at his fingertips, and an obvious pride in their accomplishments, he sketched out the chronology of the local militia.

After that introduction, Mr. Tesch gave us leave to wander at will. We climbed the massive stairs to the second floor. Nothing about this building is less than hero-sized. We found a room full of old wood paneling and leather upholstery, framed sepia photos and old political cartoons. It was like stepping back in time to an exclusive gentleman's club. The stuffed head of a large, horned black bull glared down at us from the wall. There was a gleam of weapons and uniform buttons from a row of cases along one wall. We admired swords, a well-worn knapsack, pikes and powder flasks. A tattered, charred flag labeled "Colors taken from Long Street Armory after the fire" held a place of honor.

My daughter wandered into the adjoining reading rooms with their built-in bookcases topped with gilded statues of fencers. Beyond stood a room with a yellow brick corner fireplace dated 1837-1894, the dates of the founding of the Grays and of the Armory.

I sat down in a deep leather armchair. The room was hushed; traffic noises seemed very far away. Light from the many windows glinted on a miniature brass cannon, polished to a high gloss. I suddenly realized that I wasn't alone. A handsome young man with light brown hair, parted on one side and a "crown imperial" goatee and mustache, materialized about eight feet in front of me. He was

The second-floor room where I saw the apparition
wearing a Grays uniform

wearing a Gray's uniform jacket of grey woolen material with a graduated glockenspiel pattern down the front in braid and buttons. It fit his elegant figure like a glove. He was smiling as he glided to about six feet from where I sat and then wavered away.

I was brought back to the twenty-first century by a woman's voice calling from the third floor where a caretaker has an apartment. I climbed out of the chair and my daughter and I wandered upstairs.

The third-floor bar was alive with memories. I noted brown speckled linoleum, the dark paneling hung with grim sepia WWI posters, the mannequins dressed in Vietnam- and Gulf War-era uniforms. The long narrow room had the air of a WWII canteen. Men sang, argued, and raised their glasses. The room was full, not of ghosts but with memories of comrades together.

The ballroom on the third floor was locked and I didn't want to trouble Mr. Tesch for the key. It is in the ballroom that Nick Reiter of The Avalon Foundation photographed some orbs.

A month after my visit to the Armory, Nick told me, "One of the orbs we photographed was by the place where the caretaker said he saw the figure of a soldier walk through the wall. Another was photographed in the room off the entrance downstairs where the cannon is displayed. The third was in the round tower office. I also noticed a small magnetic distortion by the door leading from the ballroom into the bar. When my magnometer readings either go up or down drastically, what it tells me is that something is either producing a magnetic field or distorting the background geomagnetic field. At the Armory, it was hard to say what it was. I wouldn't rule out a big old iron stove pipe in the wall, but it didn't seem that drastic and was actually out a little from the wall. It *appeared* to be anomalous."

Back downstairs, Mr. Tesch sat back in his chair and folded his hands.

"Yes, we have a ghost," he said deliberately. "I've been approached twice. But I don't believe in ghosts."

I looked at him quizzically.

"I believe everything is explainable. There have been a dozen sightings—mostly by people who spend more time than they should in the bar!"

At that I decided not to mention my sighting on the second floor!

"I've heard him walking behind me. I rationalize that it's an old floor and that as I walk across it, it gives way, then pops up behind me. But," he added, trying to be fair. "other people have had the same thing happen to them."

"I was working in the back. There are heavy fire doors between the auditorium and the back of the room and they always scrape when pulled shut. I heard the door scrape and went to investigate. A hand was pulling the door shut. It had gray-green skin."

Somehow this flat statement of fact was more horrifying than any emotional description could be.

He had looked out into the drill hall and he had seen no one. It is a big open room and not an easy place to hide unless the prankster was unnaturally quick.

"Now, my explanation was that we had an Administrator at that time who was over at the Armory way too much. I had the lights on. He could have seen it was me and maybe he just didn't want to say anything."

Several weeks after the hand incident, Tesch was again working in the back of the Armory. As he prepared to leave about about 11:00 p.m., he crossed the drill hall to the front door. He said he could hear footsteps behind him but there was no one visible. He is not alone in hearing the footsteps.

The Civil Air Patrol meets at the Armory. After an evening meeting, a cadet was assigned to turn out the lights in the drill hall. The switch control panel is at the front of the hall and as he walked back to the CAP rooms in the rear of the building he also heard footsteps behind him. He swore he would never be alone in the darkened drill hall again.[1]

The Civil Air Patrol was holding an officers' meeting in the first-floor turret office. A potted ficus tree, which had never been known to act in anything other than a ficus-like manner, suddenly began to shake and then toppled over in full view of the CAP commander. She shouted, "Patrick! Stop that!"[2]

No one knows where the name "Patrick" came from. A review of names listed in a book about the Grays written in 1902 revealed only one Patrick, Patrick Henry Breslin, an attorney living in Cleveland in 1859, although the book did not include a complete roster.[3]

Why *he* might haunt the Armory or want to overturn a ficus plant is a mystery. The plant was set upright and has never fallen since.

There are many additional unexplained occurrences at the Armory. Another member of the Civil Air Patrol supposedly photographed a ghostly image one winter by the Christmas tree in the lobby.

One evening, Mr. G., an associate of the CAP, and another man I'll call Sam* were cleaning up in the foyer. Mr. G. went to check that the back doors were locked and told Sam he'd circle round and meet him in front of the building in a few minutes. Sam heard him leave, then felt a cold, clammy blast of musty air coming down the grand staircase. When he looked up, he saw a man standing on the first landing. He raced out the door and almost knocked over Mr. G. He, too, swore off being in the building alone.[4]

A caretaker lives in the tower apartment. One summer the caretaker was a young college student. As he was cleaning up the grand ballroom on the third floor, he saw a man in a Grays uniform materialize through the south wall of the room between Burton Mess and the Ballroom. The ghost didn't say anything and as soon as the young man made a noise, he vanished back through the wall.[5]

Some years ago, the front lobby was being redecorated. It was painstaking work, requiring scaffolding so that the elaborate plasterwork borders could be painted. Two members were working late. It was thirsty work and they decided to take a break in the third-floor bar. While they were there, they heard footsteps coming up the grand staircase. They called out to the climber but got no answer. When they looked over the railing, no one was there. But they heard the footsteps descending the stairs. When they got back down to their scaffolding, they found that the brushes and paint pots were messily tipped over and thrown about. It was late and the building was locked.[6] Mr. Tesch shook his head over that experience.

The resident building manager hasn't seen or heard any ghosts; neither have the sound and motion detectors been tripped by anything inexplicable. I would also imagine that the presence of armed police officers in the basement firing range would be a deterrent to any pranksters or misguided ghosthunters thinking of breaking into the Armory.

Main staircase of Grays Armory

I have always admired the soldiers of the eighteenth and nineteenth centuries. Their officers led them into battle, sabers outstretched, walking unflinchingly into the face of deadly fire. Trench warfare and beachhead landings and walking point in the jungle have their own horrors. But I cannot fathom the nerve it took to face down the enemy and march in good order across a field towards certain death. There was a code of honor, of courage, of cold steel. Perhaps the young man who has been seen at the Armory died testing his courage. For over 100 years the Grays trained to be prepared, to go at a moment's notice when their country called. It may be that some long-dead duty summons the ghostly Gray to the Armory. And he stands ready to heed the call. *Semper Paratus.*

Visiting the site

Only the first floor is handicapped accessible via a ramp. There are no elevators to the second or third floors.

Your best bet for seeing most of the building is to visit it on one of Barb Zamlin's North Coast Ghost Tours. Call (330) 225-1519 for required reservations. The Armory is located right next to the historic (and reputedly haunted) Erie Street Cemetery, established in 1826. You can also go to one of the many events, including book fairs and car shows that the Armory hosts throughout the year.

Other local haunt-spots:

Drive by the arson-damaged Franklin Castle (*Haunted Ohio III*, p. 146) at W. 44th St. and Franklin Blvd. You can read the whole tragic story at http://www.franklincastle.com

Squires Castle is the site of yet another great local legend (*Haunted Ohio III*, p. 139).

Not too far away, you can visit Rider's 1812 Inn, 792 Mentor Ave, Painesville, OH 44007, (440) 354-8200 (*Haunted Ohio IV*, p. 45) where "Mistress Suzanne" keeps a watchful eye on the Inn.

Directions

Grays Armory
1234 Bolivar Road
Cleveland, OH 44115-1208
(216) 621-5938

I-71 north to E. 9th Street Exit. Go north on E. 9th. Pass Jacobs Field and just on the other side of Jacobs Field, past the Erie Street Cemetery, turn right on Bolivar. It is a one-way street. The Armory is almost to the end of Bolivar where it intersects with 14th Street.

19

IN MEMORIAM
Memorial Hall
Dayton

Death is a shadow that always follows the body.

-14th c. English proverb-

The Memorial Hall building was intended as a memorial for veterans of the Civil War but with one thing and another, it was not begun until 1907. Dedication ceremonies were held in January of 1910. The interior was renovated in 1956, a drive spurred by Miriam Rosenthal, a professional fund raiser and music lover, who was interested in improving the hall's faulty acoustics. The Hall has hosted shows from opera to gospel, boxing matches to religious revivals. It is the home to the Dayton Philharmonic Orchestra and the Dayton Opera.

Memorial Hall

HAUNT HISTORY

The lobby of Memorial Hall is coldly beautiful, like a mauso-leum, a Pantheon of Fallen Heroes. Everywhere you turn you see stained glass; acres of polished marble, bronze, and wood; memo-rial plaques and statues. A series of yellowing paintings shows men charging or marching to their deaths, soldiers bayoneted, struck by bullets, felled by illness, arrows, and cannon balls.

Concert-goers in their finery, sipping white wine or busy being seen on the balcony, rarely give the faded battle scenes a glance. For them Memorial Hall is a bustling place, thronged with the living, home to the opera and orchestra. Few of them realize it is also home to at least one dead man, the man I call "Drake." And it is a curious thing that in a place with so many memorials to the dead, there is not even a plaque to his memory.

The Auditorium itself is designed in a bland early-60s style I can only describe as *Ed-Sullivan-Show*-Moderne. It is said that there isn't a bad seat in the house. Except for the one the Memorial ghost found himself in many years ago. "Drake" (*Haunted Ohio*, p. 56) was working at Memorial when he fell off the stage into the orches-tra pit. He died of complications from the fall and has been unable to tear himself away from the theatre ever since.

When I called the Stagehand's Union, Office Manager Mary Hughes said, "Ghost stories? I probably know some myself." And she told me the following story:

"I have a friend named Harriet. She's receptive to that stuff. I'm not. She grew up in a house near Latrobe, Pennsylvania, that they think was part of the Underground Railroad. She hates the house! In the night she'd hear somebody coming up the front stairway, walking like somebody with a peg leg. Then she'd wake up to see two people standing at the foot of the bed!

"About a year ago, my friend and her husband had tickets for a show at Memorial Hall. Their seats were in the balcony and since the house was so full and there weren't enough restrooms, the balcony seats were told they could use the stage right Chorus Dressing Room. This is clear up at the top of the hall by the bal-cony. It's just a cubbyhole with one stall, a sink, and a dressing area."

Harriet phoned Mary within a day of the show. Mary asked her how she had liked it. Her friend commented about the long bathroom lines and how the balcony patrons had been directed to the alternate bathrooms.

"'Mary,' she told me. 'I took my turn in the stall and I swear there was someone in there with me.'

"'Harriet, you're kidding me,' I said. I mean, we're talking a *small* stall. 'Where was this person or thing?'

"'At my left side, by my head.'

"'You're sure?'

"'I'm as serious as the devil!' Harriet said. 'It didn't scare me; it just gave me the weirdest feeling. *He* was scared.'

"I burst out laughing. 'You don't know about Drake?'

"'Who's Drake?'

"'That's the Memorial Hall ghost.' I'd never told her the tale."

Mary realized that those dressing rooms normally would not have been used for this particular show.

"Poor Drake thought he was safe in there! And here come all these women traipsing in and out and he's stuck!"

Mary says that she's not scared of the dead man. Still, she told me, "If there's no one in the building, Mary takes a holiday. Me and Drake are not going to sit and hold hands all day!"

Betty Rice used to be Memorial Hall's building manager.

"I was there seven days a week. For twelve years, I would have to lock up at nights." Usually she would make her rounds with a security or maintenance man; then they would leave together about midnight. But occasionally, perhaps three nights a week, she would be alone in the building, locking up on her own.

"You know those grey inside doors going into the auditorium from the hallway? They're heavy doors and they make a noise when they open—a kind of a click from the hinge. I was walking down the aisle inside the auditorium, checking to see if the lights were out, when I heard a click from this one door. It felt like someone was watching me. This happened a lot—even though I *knew* there was nobody there but me, I turned and watch the door swing shut.

"When I started work I heard about the ghost stories from the stage manager. There are never any problems during a performance but when I'm there by myself, in the dark, the house lights go on, just for a couple of seconds, then they go off again. Or just one light in a circuit will go on, which is impossible from an electrical point of view. Sometimes it felt like they were putting on a private show, just for me!"

In the hallway, just outside the auditorium, Betty was talking to a maintenance staff member while another colleague stood by. There were no doors open, but she felt a cold draft whisk past her. "We just kind of looked at each other; we both understood." Normally, Betty says, the hallways are warm, summer or winter.

"One night after one of our Gospel concerts, I was in the aisle towards the orchestra pit and I had that feeling, like I was being watched. I turned around and saw a shadow, like the silhouette of a tall man walking up in the balcony. And then there wasn't anybody there. There was no sense of evil. It was more protective, watching out for me. I saw it just once. It was about six foot two, medium build, and it moved very slowly, almost in slow motion. It only lasted a couple of seconds, maybe five seconds at the most. I wasn't scared, just surprised. 'Who in the world is that?' I thought. Then it was gone. I just kind of stood there. 'Oh, I know what that was,' I said. But I did go up in the balcony, just to check."

Some energy does seem to be floating around the balcony. It was early June, 2000 when I visited. The auditorium wasn't completely dark. The "ghost light" had been left on on stage and there were dim ceiling lights on above the balcony. Betty had assured me the stagehands had all gone home so I wouldn't be bothered. I was visiting just to take photos, but I got the usual punch in the pit of my stomach.

"Oh, there *is* someone in here," I thought, as I saw the silhouette of a man standing by what seemed to be a light board. I walked down the aisle a little further and looked back. I had been mistaken. As I stood by the orchestra pit and scanned the house, I again saw a shadowy man, standing in the right far corner. I looked again. No, nobody there.

I took some photos, not really having much hope that anything could show up without more light. Yet, in all of the photos of the balcony I took, I kept thinking, if only I was a little taller I might have been able to capture the top of someone's head, standing down in the access ramps, on tiptoe, peering at me.

That evening at my computer I went through the balcony photos painstakingly cropping and enlarging. I was getting tired and

Memorial Hall balcony orb

I almost skipped the last photo. On the very last shot of the left balcony, I found an orb hanging like a soap bubble above the exit sign. A projection from my own mind? Something seeping out of the walls? Or, perhaps, Drake?

Although a silhouette-man in the balcony is unnerving enough, Betty has also heard a ghostly whispered conversation in the Cabaret Room, a small rehearsal room seating about 300 people. It sounds like a couple of people whispering together, always very late at night after the performers and staff have gone home.

Betty told me, "I've even gone down into the basement thinking

Who in the world indeed? Or who out of it? And one wonders: whom or *what* has Drake found to talk to?

Visiting the site

Memorial Hall is fully handicapped accessible. See p. 69 and p. 162 for other local haunt-spots.

Directions

Memorial Hall
125 E. First St.
Dayton, OH 45402
(937) 224-9000

Take I-75 to First Street exit and go east towards downtown.

Memorial Hall soldier statue

Mansfield Memorial Museum

THE MUSEUM TIME FORGOT
Mansfield Memorial Museum
Mansfield

We two kept house, the Past and I,
The past and I;
I tended while it hovered nigh,
Leaving me never alone.

-Thomas Hardy-

The massive building was built as a veteran's meeting place in 1889 by the Cleveland Stone Company of local stone. Known as the Soldiers and Sailors Memorial Building, it is the oldest continuously used veteran's building in Ohio. The downstairs held the Richland County Library from 1889-1907, with a reading room in a front room, and the stacks in the rear. An opera house, which stood behind the building, burned in 1929. There were no fatalities in the fire, but two men were killed when twenty-five tons of brick fell on them as they were inspecting the wreckage. Twenty feet was taken off the back of the Soldier and Sailors building to enlarge the lot for the Madison Theatre.

The original Mansfield Memorial Museum whose mission was "preservation and education" was housed on the third floor. It was the brain-child of Mr. Edward Wilkinson, a tinner by trade. Wilkinson was one of those self-taught working-man naturalists the Victorian era produced in such quantities. He was trained as a geologist and in the late 1860s to mid-1870s he traveled as an "acquisioner"—a collector of specimens for the Smithsonian Institution. He visited Mexico to work in his aunt's silver mine and collected specimens for the Field Museum in Chicago, the Peabody, and the Carnegie. Wilkinson was recognized as the pre-eminent naturalist of the Midwest. He often asked other fellow enthusiasts like Dr. J.W. Craig to bring specimens home from their travels, perhaps casually asking, "While you're in Australia, would you mind picking me up an emu?"

From 1889 to 1897, some 65,000 people came through the Museum—this at a time when the entire population of Mansfield was only 14,000. Hailed as the premier museum in the Midwest, it was *the* place to visit. The building was never locked and the curator has had older people tell him about visiting the Museum as children, then running over to the Madison Theatre for a matinee.

Wilkinson died in 1918 of arsenic poisoning. It was rumored that he was poisoned by the arsenic solutions used to preserve the Museum's stuffed animals but he actually died from inhaling the arsenic given off in tin processing.

After his death, a local scoutmaster organized the local children who cleaned glass, dusted, and swept from the 1920s until 1955 when, Victorian museums having fallen out of fashion, the Museum was closed. It was closed for forty-four years—until Scott Schaut came to town.

"I found the Museum by accident. I have a background in museum work and had come from Washington where real estate is so expensive. I was looking for something I could afford and bought a house in Sherman's Estate. As I was doing some research, I found a picture labeled "Edward Wilkinson, Director and Curator, Mansfield Memorial Museum" in the 1896 *Richland County Atlas.*

"I asked around about the Museum and was told that it had been closed for years. Some local people told me not to bother to try to see the museum because it had been stripped of all valuable items and only contained some insects and stuffed birds."

Scott persisted, going back repeatedly until he found one of the Board members, Mr. Gib Fronz, in the building.

"He look me upstairs through all of the cobwebs and I couldn't believe what I was seeing. I was in Heaven! It was as if the museum was frozen in time from before the museum had closed. Every week for eight months I was allowed to go to the museum and just look at all of the artifacts and history that had been shut away."

Scott inherited a treasure-trove of chaos. Another fire had swept through the Museum in 1986 when the old Madison Theatre was being torn down. Most of the collection was coated in soot. A Civil War-era print hangs in the Museum. Half of it has been cleaned; the other half is covered with a black film of soot. It is a graphic illustration of the massive cleanup Scott has accomplished.

In November 1997 Scott was appointed Director and Curator for Life by the Board in recognition for his commitment to the Museum. The Museum reopened on Memorial Day 1999.

HAUNT HISTORY

When I heard about the museum in the Soldiers and Sailors Memorial, I expected to find a grubby local military museum full of dusty displays of rusted minie ball fragments with fly-specked signs: "Dug up on Gettysburg Battlefield." Instead I found a cabinet of curiosities, a Victorian museum that time forgot.

I climbed the massive stairs to the second floor and found a young man in shorts and hiking boots brushing stain on a display case. With his clean-shaven good looks he could have posed for a turn-of-the-century illustrator of strong-jawed young men in stiff collars and tennis flannels. After a few cordialities, he waved me around the corner to the museum.

At the door, I was stunned to find myself back in the nineteenth century. Spiky egrets and spinning wheels were silhouetted on top of wooden display cases in the late-afternoon light. A snowy, skull-faced barn owl glared at me from a case by the door. I barely had time to take it all in before I was hit with a body blow that doubled me over. Glancing to my left, something in a frame caught my fragmented attention.

Mansfield Memorial Museum
main exhibit room

It was a shattered, crumpled drum head, labeled "Drumhead found on the Battlefield of Gettysburg, 1863."

Somehow I found myself at the other end of the room by a black-draped memorial wreath for President Garfield, clutching a radiator cover, sobbing tearlessly, and trying to not let anyone hear me. I was torn by dry heaves as I tried to compose myself.

"Get a grip," I told myself. The floor was trembling. I forced myself to straighten up, to circle the room, to methodically take notes. It was a high-ceilinged room with wonderful out-of-period deco lamps. The floor was ocean-blue linoleum, bordered in red and white.

I started beside a bare tree trunk labeled, "planted by Johnny Appleseed." Here was a handmade wooden cash register. There was the lower jaw of a tiger owned by P.T. Barnum, and a circus drum. At this point I noticed I was not alone. Looking at the notes I wrote that day, I see that I underscored the word "BOY" so deeply that the pen nearly went through the paper.

From time to time, I glanced fearfully at the row of cases containing military uniforms. It was from them that the disturbance seemed to come. I continued to take notes, my shoulders hunched. Ice Age-era wood, a mastodon's jaw bone, Philippine be-heading swords, the frock coat of Senator John Sherman, who ran for president in 1888. A velocipede or "bone shaker" bicycle made by the Museum's director Mr. Wilkinson in 1868 shared a case with a moth-eaten parrot, "27 years old at the time of death" and sheets of 1846 wallpaper.

Every artifact competed for my attention: stockings from the Revolutionary War, a plait of hair labeled in Wilkinson's hand: "relic of Johnstown flood," botanical specimens pressed flat behind glass, the original chain and compass used to survey Richland County.

The collection included stuffed animals and birds of every description including costumed ducks and a rooster sitting around a Victorian tea table. One case was full of guns taken by John Brown from the Harper's Ferry Armory as well as the most unique piece in the Museum: a pike, or spear-like weapon, one of 1,000 made by Brown to arm the slaves he intended to free in the uprising.

"Only three of these are known to exist," Scott told me later. "Even the Smithsonian doesn't have one."

There seems to be nothing that Wilkinson did not collect. It is an amazing, eclectic collection, all housed in period wooden cases that are as marvelous as their contents. When the Smithsonian held a grand exposition in 1876 in honor of the country's centennial, they designed a series of elegant wood and glass display cases. When Mr. Wilkinson wrote for information on setting up his Museum, the Smithsonian sent him the plans for the centennial cases.

A woman's voice brought me back to this century. A couple—he tall and tattooed; she, short, breathless, and shrill—

The Gettysburg drum head

swirled into the hall and disrupted the energies that had been overwhelming me. I was irritated, yet thankful at the same time.

I was completely exhausted. I walked out of the main Museum room, past a case of Zulu spears and stuffed monkeys, past a rainbow of birds arranged in a smaller case and sank into a chair by the steps. So many men, so many wars, I thought. I could hardly hold up my head.

It was then that I got my first clear look at the ghostly boy. My first impression was the 1860s-70s period. He was wearing short knee pants (not fitted at the knee like knickers) and a short jacket over a white shirt. His clothes were casual and coarse rather than dress-up clothes. He was about eight or nine years old and he was bright and shiny as a new penny. He clambered up the stairs towards the third floor, smiling back at me, beckoning to me to follow. The stairs were blocked by a padlocked grill.

I was too drained to get up. Getting the key to the third floor meant walking all the way down the stairs to the first floor to fetch Scott. I just sat there staring at the stuffed moose head on the landing. The little boy put his fingers into his mouth and whistled to get my attention. Then he was upstairs. He had melted past the grill and was pressing his face to the stair rails, making faces at me. I smiled in spite of myself.

"Cheeky little monkey," I thought.

When Scott returned, I finally hoisted myself out of the chair. He unlocked the grill and climbed the stairs ahead of me. As I rounded the curve to the next flight of steps, the little boy slipped his hand into mine and led me upstairs. When we got to the top, he stepped back and stood there, looking pleased. Then he disappeared.

It was like King Tut's tomb: I could see the original stenciled wall decoration, the paint lighter where it had been hidden and preserved by a huge case. The enormous curved wooden truss, six layers of wood thick, that holds up the entire building. A stuffed peacock sprawled atop a tall case. "The moths got at the tail feathers," Scott remarked. "There's a local man who raises peacocks. I'm going to ask him for feathers to replace them."

The entire Museum was originally housed on this floor. But the Fire Marshall told Scott that he would have to move the displays down to the second floor since there was only one way in and out of the third floor. All the cases with their original glass had to be taken apart since they were too large to be moved in one piece.

"We only broke one pane moving the cases, and that was *my* fault," Scott confessed. "The rest of the glass is completely original."

The move seemed to agitate the ghost, which Scott feels may be Edward Wilkinson, whose life was devoted to the Museum.

"When I first got here, I felt like the mood was, 'what are you doing?' We had to dismantle the cases, move them, reassemble them. You're looking at three and a half years work. But as soon as I finished reassembling the cases, the mood changed from worry to contentment."

Back downstairs in the second-floor Museum room, Scott pointed at a framed photo of a bearded man who looks very pleased.

"That's Edward Wilkinson's picture. It hung on the third floor. When we started moving things down and this room was empty, I took the picture and hung it first thing in this room. I swear to God, he wasn't smiling when we first brought it down...

"There have been two sightings of a man. The first was when we had just put the cases in. There were no artifacts in them yet. I was standing at the third uniform case. It was about this time of day [5:00 p.m.] and I could see the west windows reflected in the case windows. I saw the shadow of a man, passing from left to right. There were no details, just an adult-sized man's shadow. It lasted about fifteen seconds.

"The other time, a volunteer was downstairs in the library reading room and saw a shadow go past the doorway.

"But I've also heard him sneeze. It was the middle of winter. There was some noise, the building creaking, etc., but all the windows were shut. I was sitting by the front desk when I heard a sneeze from upstairs. Sound travels very well down the stairwell. Of course, I went right upstairs. 'Hello?' I said, 'Is anybody there?' Of course, nobody was there.

"About four hours later on the same day I went into the reading room of the library and I heard it again from upstairs. Both of sneezes were a man's sneeze, rather muffled.

"I'm not the only one who hears things. I was working in the basement while a pair of volunteers, a man and a woman, were sitting at the desk in the front hall. They heard steps, first on the second floor, then going up to the third floor. Then I came up from the basement." The couple was completely shocked.

"How did you get past us?" they asked Scott.

"I told them that I hadn't been upstairs at all, that I'd been in the basement the whole time. I said that it was just Mr. Wilkinson checking the museum and the building like he always does."

In the years while the Museum was closed, board members would sometimes be there alone, dusting. They'd hear footsteps or noises realistic enough to make them think that another board member had come into the building. They would walk down to the first floor, but never find anyone there. There was always the feeling of *somebody* being around.

As I was shouldering my camera to leave, I suddenly realized that I hadn't taken a photo of Mr. Wilkinson. Scott stayed behind as I dashed up the stairs. As I turned left in the hall, I caught a glimpse of someone behind me and jumped about a foot. Then I realized that there was no one there and scolded myself for letting my imagination run away with me.

Back downstairs, I told Scott that I was getting imaginative. He smiled. "Oh, that happens all the time: people thinking that someone is right behind them."

I don't know why I didn't see or sense Mr. Wilkinson, unless it was he who was behind me when I went upstairs to take his photo. The little boy is a mystery, unless he is somehow attached to the drumhead, which seems to have triggered it all. He did not wear a uniform and I did not get the impression that he was a drummer boy. Perhaps he is the Spirit of the Museum, representing the thousands of children who have walked these halls, exclaiming over the emu, awed by the guns, giggling at the stuffed ducks at tea.

My Aunt had relatives in Mansfield, in fact, her cousin was married in the church directly across the street from the Museum, but she was puzzled when I described it. "There's a Museum there? What does the building look like? Has it always been there?"

"That's the trouble," Scott said ruefully. "We've been closed for so long people have forgotten us. It's easy just to walk by."

He pointed out the heavy original woodwork, the wormy chestnut paneling in the basement, and told how the original iron chandeliers had been donated to a WWII metal drive.

"We've got all the original woodwork. We're very lucky. The good thing about the building having been closed for so long is that nobody remodeled it "

When I asked Scott what his favorite artifact was he first mentioned a collection of children's artwork from 1901. "They're pieces of time, stopped." Another favorite is the Johnny Appleseed tree. Scott had no idea of its significance when he first came to the Museum, since the label had been lost.

"When we first opened, a gentleman in his nineties approached me. He told me that he used to help out at the Museum.

"'Too bad you don't have those trees anymore,' he said. 'I remember having to dust those damn trees.'

"'Really?' I said. 'Why is it too bad?'

"'Because Johnny Appleseed planted them.'

"Well, we had those trees. We just didn't know what they were. The trees had been planted between 1812 and 1815. There were two pieces—a large trunk and a smaller piece.

"'Every time I dusted,' said the old gentleman, 'a piece of bark fell off!'

"So we were able to label them and put them back on display," Scott finished with satisfaction.

Scott has many plans for the future.

"We've got minerals and fossils that are not on display yet. I think we've got the nicest collection of seashells in the state. The insects are also not on display. We've got thirteen species of extinct birds and a beautiful skull collection. We are always looking to enlarge our collections, particularly photos, clothing and other historical memorabilia from Mansfield and Richland County and we are interested in foreign and American military items as well as guns."

Eventually Scott wants to put the twenty feet back on the building, add an elevator, and a repository room on the third floor, where specimens can be stored until needed for loan or display. I complimented Scott on a truly unique museum experience. "We've come a long way in a short period of time," he said.

"This Museum was Mr. Wilkinson's life—his legacy to the community. It is now *my* life and, in my small way, my legacy to leave for future generations. I tell people that when I die I want to be cremated and the ashes put on the third floor. And if anything is changed I'll come out of the woodwork, like *Poltergeist*, and haunt the place!"

Visiting the site

The second floor is not currently handicapped accessible. The first floor, which is dedicated to military history, is accessible via a ramp.

See p. 12 for more information about the Mansfield area.

Directions

Mansfield Memorial Museum
34 Park Ave. West
Mansfield, OH 44902
(419) 525-2491

Located next to the Bank One building (north side) one block west from the city square on Park Avenue.

21

A SPIRIT RISES
The Victoria Theatre
Dayton

A pretty girl is like a melody that haunts you night and day.

-Irving Berlin-

David Hastings, Senior House Manager at the Victoria Theatre, was enthusiastic when I called him about this book. David has a flair for fun, an irrepressible zest for life, whether he's dashing across the lobby to turn on the house lights or feeding Sugar Babies™ to a police horse on the sidewalk in front of the Victoria's grand glass doors.

But he takes very seriously what he calls, "our beautiful energy," otherwise known as "Miss Victoria," the ghost of the Victoria Theatre.

The Victoria Theatre, Dayton

She was an actress who, sometime in the late 1800s, disappeared mysteriously from her dressing room. One moment she was seen going back to her dressing room for a forgotten fan. The next, the Stage Manager was pounding frantically on her door. When they forced their way in, she was gone. She has not been seen in the flesh since. But her rose perfume drifts down the staircases at the Victoria. She has been known to brush by people on the stairs and rustles her taffeta petticoats in the darkened balcony.

Miss Victoria is just one supernatural manifestation at the Victoria. Another strange tale involves one of the "opera boxes," those plush-lined, gilt-edged balconies on either side of the stage. A young woman was assaulted by a madman in the house-left box* in the late 1800s. She was not killed, but the horror of that insane attack still lingers. Anyone who enters the box with anger or a bad attitude will find the temperature in the box becomes frosty. Some have even said they have been slapped by an invisible energy.

"The energy hasn't been there since the renovation in 1990," David told me. But recently some part of it seems to have revived.

In the first part of May 2000, the Victoria was presenting *The Red Balloon*, one of its "Discovery Shows," for school children. The theatrical troupe had just arrived from Canada that morning. They immediately started setting up and rehearsing. No one told them anything about the ghosts. The luxurious opera boxes proved irresistible to one of the actresses. She climbed the narrow stairs to the house left box, opened the swinging door, and made herself comfortable in an armchair lushly upholstered in green velvet.

The woman watched the cast warm-up for a while, then got up to leave. When she pushed at the door, it didn't budge. She tried again. Then she began to laugh. Obviously one of her fellow cast members was playing a prank.

"Would someone please come up and unlock the door," she called down to the actors on stage.

"Those doors don't lock," called a stagehand.

The actress threw her whole body weight against it. "Well, it won't *op*-en!" she said, more amused than angry.

Rick Flynn, Customer Services Manager, was on hand. He went up to the door to the box and opened it effortlessly. He said that

---

* The box on the left, as you are facing the stage.

Victoria Theatre opera box

the door swung freely. There was no way it could have swelled or been wedged shut.

That same day Rick had trouble with the TV stage monitor in the lobby. Despite repeated tests showing that it was in perfect working order, it remained dark. Finally, some minutes into the show, the monitor mysteriously switched on. Just another one of Miss Victoria's little pranks?

The way some of the staff talks about the ghost, you'd think she was some amusingly eccentric stage legend, a slightly dotty actress whose foibles are legendary. A persona has built up for the ghostly lady: a mysterious and delightfully feminine presence with definite likes and dislikes.

"She *loves* the elevator," David confided. "Anyone who's here in the evening will tell you that one of her favorite things is to play with the elevator."

The elevator in question with its highly polished brass doors is just across the hall from David's office. The elevator is adjusted so that it always returns to the first floor. When it does, its doors don't open unless there is a passenger. After hours David locks down the elevator so that no one can go up in it, only descend from the upper floors. He regularly hears the elevator come to life, making a distinctively creepy creaking sound. It goes up to the second or sometimes the third floor, the door opens, then "someone or *some-*

thing" pushes the "Down" button. The elevator comes back down to the first floor and the door opens so an invisible passenger can alight. When David hears it, he sometimes rolls his chair back to where he can see the door open and *nobody* walk out.

"Sometimes I'll leave at 4 p.m., then come back around 7 p.m. so I can get some work done with no interruptions," David told me. "She's just up and down, up and down, all night! The elevator maintenance man is baffled by the whole thing."

Miss Victoria has continued her legendary performances throughout the theatre. Staff frequently smell her perfume. The Property Management Staff is used to hearing her slam doors in the bathrooms when they're cleaning. She also turns off the lights in the bathrooms, when you least expect it. "She *enjoys* the bathrooms," David said. Rick also told of being startled by a flush in a stall he knew was empty, even though the toilet was not an automatic model.

It was in the second-floor ladies room where, early in the morning, a cleaner saw the apparition of a headless, armless woman in a black dress walk out of a bathroom stall before her startled eyes. I tried to photograph the area for this book. The bathroom is all green marble and mirrors and I couldn't get a good shot of anything. There were too many reflections. I leaned back for just one more shot. The lights went out. My heart stopped.

"Just *slide* backwards to the door," I thought, fighting down panic. "You can be out of here in a second..." Then I suddenly realized that I had backed into the light switch.

I told in *Haunted Ohio* (p. 58) of how a cameraman and anchorwoman heard a rustling from the empty balcony, like someone in a long dress walking by. Miss Victoria hasn't forgotten her balcony haunt.

David told me, "Last winter [2000] I was in the theatre late. I was up in the balcony with my friend Ed, checking to see that the emergency doors were closed. The house lights were all off except the 'ghost light' on stage. We were standing at the front left side of the balcony. I heard giggling. It was just a little half-laugh, a snicker up by the emergency exit. We could see that no one was there. Ed froze. 'Who's in here?' he demanded.

"No one," David said casually.

"I just heard someone laugh!" said his friend.

"So did I," David said, and explained about Miss Victoria.

"GHOSTS!" Ed exclaimed. He was badly frightened and insisted on leaving immediately.

Miss Victoria remains "the beautiful energy" at the Victoria Theatre. You may feel her brushing by you on the grand staircases or catch the faintest hint of her fragrance as she drifts by. But why doesn't she retire from this theatrical haunting? Why does she rustle through balcony and bathroom? Why does she amuse herself with childish games like riding the elevator? That, I fear, will have to remain Miss Victoria's secret.

Visiting the site

There are automatic doors and elevators. There is also wheelchair seating. Interpreters are also available by request.

The Theatre hosts a variety of series including the Broadway series (the area's largest), Theatre for the Young at Heart, Next Stage, and Opera series, and my personal favorite: Hot Times—Cool Films, a summer classic film series which includes a pre-movie theatre organ concert and a cartoon with the film for a back-to-your-childhood movie experience.

See p. 69 and p. 146 for more Dayton haunt-spots.

Directions

Victoria Theatre Association
138 N Main St.
Dayton, OH 45459-4647
(937) 228-7591

Web site: www.victoriatheatre.com

I-75 to W. First Street Exit. Go east on W. First Street to N. Main. The Theatre is at the intersection of N. Main and W. First.

22

TWO SPIRITED WOMEN
Kelton House
Columbus

...she knew the whole duty of womankind,
To take the burden and have the power
And seem like the well-protected flower,
To manage a dozen industries
With a casual gesture in scraps of ease,
To hate the sin and to love the sinner
And to see that the gentlemen got their dinner...
-Stephen Vincent Benet, *John Brown's Body (1927)*-

Fernando Cortez Kelton and Sophia Stone Kelton built this house in 1852. The Keltons were active members of the local antislavery society. Family tradition states that runaways were hidden in the barn at the back of the house, in the 300-barrel cistern just east of the house or sometimes in the servants' quarters.

Sophia Kelton experienced many tragedies in her life. Her son Charles died at age two. Oscar Kelton, the Kelton's eldest son, enlisted in the Union Army against his parents' wishes. He was killed at the battle of Brice's Crossroads at Guntown, Mississippi in June of 1864. His comrades hastily buried his body, marking the spot with a wooden sign fixed to a tree with a bayonet. About a year and a half later, Fernando Kelton learned that the grave of his son had been marked and decided to bring his body home. He traveled to Mississippi, exhumed the partially decomposed body and began the trip back to the train with the coffin in a farm wagon. The wagon hit a rut and overturned, spilling the grisly contents of the coffin and throwing Fernando onto his head. He never really recovered from the shock or the head injuries, which left him dizzy, weak, and with terrible headaches.[1]

In 1866, back in Columbus in his business office downtown, Fernando was suddenly struck with a dizzy spell. He staggered over to the open window for air, lost his balance, and fell three stories to the pavement. He was carried back to Kelton House, where he died in the four-poster bed still shown there today. Sophia died in 1888.

After Sophia's death, the house passed to Frank Kelton and his wife Isabella. They traded houses with Frank's brother Edwin and his wife Laura who had five daughters and needed a larger house. Edwin and Laura's daughter, Grace Bird Kelton, inherited the house and she lived there until her death in 1974.

Grace Bird Kelton willed the house to the Columbus Foundation with the request that they find someone to restore the house into a museum. She stipulated that the Foundation had a year to do it, and if no one could be found to take over the house, it was to be torn down and the grounds made into a park. The Junior League of Columbus accepted the challenge and has been administering Kelton House for twenty-five years. The house is a popular spot for weddings and special events.

HAUNT HISTORY

Kelton House's façade is decorously clad in dull brick, the very image of a prosperous, soberly clothed nineteenth-century gentleman, its only extravagance the wrought-iron balcony, like a fancy waistcoat.

A Victorian gentleman's house was meant to display his wealth and taste. His wife's domain was the house and it was no mean task to run it, to judge by Sophia's detailed account books. She managed the servants, ordered provisions, saw to the laundry, the linens, and the coal. She made sure food was properly served and entertained guests. She might go from attending a sick servant to overseeing the dressmaking to pouring tea for her guests or arranging an evening musicale. All this while wearing corsets and a hoop!

On my recent visit to Kelton House I found the taste of an upper-class Victorian family lushly displayed throughout the house. Kelton House Director Georgeanne Reuter and Special Events Coordinator Mark Mann pointed out various details and filled me in on the history. The huge gilt-framed console mirrors over the carved marble fireplaces in the front and back parlors were found for the house by Jim Williams of Savannah's *Midnight in the Garden of Good and Evil* fame, a consultant on the house's décor. The parlor windows were framed by heavy gold brocade curtains. By a mirrored whatnot shelf hung a portrait of Oscar Kelton in his Union uniform, doing his best to appear fierce and military, the merest ghost of a mustache on his upper lip. A candle from the whatnot shelf threw a bayonet-sharp shadow on the wall next to his portrait.

Sophia Kelton

The décor is pure Victorian opulence, tempered with Sophia Kelton's shrewd thrift. Mark pointed out that the valences in the two parlors were actually parts of a bed taken to pieces and made up by the local carpenter.

Across the hall was a less formal parlor. The chairs and settees were child-sized. Sophia was a tiny woman. She directed her carpenter to cut down the legs on all of her furniture. One can't play the dignified hostess if one's feet are dangling. This parlor contained many little things under glass: a collection of china cottages used as incense burners, a pale wreath of delicate shell flowers quivering on wires. A blown-glass fantasia of a bird and fountain under a glass dome. In a glass case sits a scrapbook compiled by Anna Kelton, the Kelton's oldest daughter. She had literary ambitions, not to be countenanced in a girl of her era and social prominence. The scrapbook tells of author readings attended, favorite poems and unfulfilled yearnings.

Oddly enough, it is not Oscar or Fernando Kelton, their lives cut tragically short, who are most frequently reported at Kelton House. Instead, it is the haunt of two strong-willed and extraordinary women. Sophia lived her life under the constraints of her time as "the Angel in the House," the revered maternal figure, serenely unaware of the unpleasant things of life. But Sophia, who opened her house to fugitive slaves, was no china doll. When she found a sick ten-year-old slave in the bushes, she cared for her until she was well. The girl spent the next ten years living at Kelton House and in 1874 she married the Kelton's cabinetmaker in the front parlor.

Sophia was also no fool. She once installed a billiard table in the front parlor to keep her sons home at night. She knew very well that they weren't going out to play billiards but she also knew that they would never dare admit the sordid truth to her.

Grace Bird Kelton, on the other hand, had no problem flouting society and its conventions. She seems to have been a flamboyant "Auntie Mame"-type character. She was an independent, unmarried woman at a time when women were still expected to defer to men. She trained as an artist in New York, then took up interior design before it was a recognized profession. She traveled extensively well into her eighties, and designed interiors for clients all over the world.

Always an exceedingly stylish dresser, as an old lady Grace dyed her hair red, dressed all in red, and drove a red car. One Columbus fireman remembered how he had been dispatched to Kelton House on Christmas Day, 1969, solely to carry Grace, who would then have been eight-nine or ninety years old, from the second floor to the first so she could receive her visitors.

In the hall I admired an antique tallcase clock from Sophia's dowry. A clipper ship silhouette cut out of metal, rocked furiously upon a painted ocean. Just beyond was the staircase with its beautifully carved newel post. The foot of this stair was the site of an unforgettable ghostly encounter.

Mark played me a tape that was made in 1998 at a Docent/Staff dinner as the guests shared personal Kelton House ghost stories. Many of the incidents reported related to the Columbus Landmarks Foundation Halloween Tours. It seems as though the energy supplied by the people who flow through the house somehow "charges up" the building.

The 1994 Halloween tour was over and the volunteers were closing up the house. Melissa* turned off the lights and was walking from the kitchen towards the front door with another volunteer, Doug*. Doug, whom Melissa called "quite theatrical," was going on about "the midnight hour, the full moon, witches, warlocks, etc. etc."

Sick of it, Melissa turned her head to tell Doug to shut up. Just as she passed the bottom of the stairs, she walked smack into someone, catching the impact on her right cheek. She said it felt like someone taller than her five foot four inches wearing a soft, cottony shirt. She leaped back, thinking she had run into a leftover tour guest and started to apologize.

Then she realized that there was nobody there. She backed into Doug, who was still coming along the hall.

Sophia's Room

"What happened?" asked Doug.

"I just walked into somebody!" said Melissa. Utterly shocked, she retreated down the hall and refused to leave through the front door.

On the tape Melissa said, "I thought it was a male guest! It was a complete surprise!"

And then came a shock of my own. A voice close to the microphone whispered, "Yes."

I began to feel like Bruce Willis in *The Sixth Sense*. I played the tape back over and over. My daughter heard it too: a creepy little whispery voice that said, "yes" over the background noise. Of course I wasn't there when the session was taped. It might have been someone in the room responding to a question. But it sounds like the speaker's lips are right next to the microphone.

Ghostly whispers are nothing new at Kelton House.

One guest on a Landmarks Foundation Tour came to Joyce* afterwards and complained, "It was very rude of the house to hide someone in the closet!"

Puzzled, Joyce asked her to explain. The guest had been in the parlor with the three tour guides and a group of other guests when she heard somebody whispering to her from the closet. It sounded like an older man. But the tour guides were the only people in the building besides the guests and the closet was so crammed full of chairs that no one could possibly get inside it to play a prank.

One docent, closing up after the bus tour, was up on the third floor. He locked the door behind him and started down the stairs.

"I was just sort of saying goodnight to the house," he said. "Suddenly, clear and sweet as can be, in my left ear, I heard a very feminine voice say, 'Good evening.'

Upstairs, Sophia's room was arranged for the summer, with cool straw mats on the floor replacing the carpets which would have been taken up, beaten clean and stored until fall. The bed and mirror were shrouded in ghostly white netting like the mad Miss Havisham in her wedding veil. There were no window screens in Sophia's day. The bed net kept off flying pests and the mirror drape kept flies from speckling the glass. It was in this bedroom that some of the most chilling sightings of Sophia's ghost have taken place.

One evening, a volunteer called Renee* left after closing up the empty house. As she waited in her car to pull out of the driveway, she glanced up at the window of "Sophia's Room" overlooking Town Street. She saw someone in the window, dressed in black with something like a veil over its head. The figure did not seem completely solid but Renee thought, "I locked somebody in the house!" She went back in and searched but found no one. She drove home thinking, "I know that person. I've seen a picture or something…"

The next day she came back wondering if there was something in the upstairs window that could have given the illusion of a figure. She searched the room and stared at the window from every angle but there was nothing. Coming back down the stairs, she suddenly made the connection. There on the wall in front of her, was the portrait of Sophia Kelton with her black dress and wings of black hair. "That's her!" she exclaimed.

Kelton House dining room

A short time after this sighting, the house manager confided to Renee, "I don't know if I can stay here." She explained that, "A woman was looking out of the window at me after I left." Renee asked her to describe the figure. It was the same woman, dressed in black, with black hair. And not only did the house manager see it but her roommate, who had come to meet her, saw the figure also. They both thought it was a living human being. Mark feels that it is only right that Sophia Kelton should see off her guests from the window. "This was *her* house," he said "and she's not given the place up yet!"

Docent Paul* said that, after he finished the tours on October 31, 1996, he drifted upstairs and stood in the door of Sophia's room. There he saw an image of a woman like a bust on a pedestal. It seemed to be made of "milky smoke." He couldn't make out any features. He only saw that it was wearing a long dress. Paul came racing downstairs almost incoherent with shock. His fellow docents said he was as white as a ghost himself.

But Sophia does not confine herself to her own room. Mark Mann's wife has seen a small woman dressed in black on the back stairs. My daughter may have glimpsed her in the dining room.

In the dining room, the peachbloom velvet curtains trimmed with gold fringe, glowed rosily in the late afternoon sunlight under their carved gilt valances. Lace curtains flowed over the vibrant carpet. The crystal, silver, and old wood subtly spoke of Money, gotten in Trade perhaps, but still property of a gentleman. I was especially fascinated by the Sheraton sideboard of richly polished mahogany with its rolltop tambours and slots to hold the silverware. Over the sideboard hung an oval portrait of a lady wearing a bow-shaped brooch made of human hair. The brooch itself, found in the attic, sat framed on the sideboard.

As I scribbled notes by the stairs, I shooed my daughter down the hall. I had told her nothing about Kelton House and there is very little in my first book about the sightings of Sophia. She came whizzing back in a few minutes, big-eyed.

She told me, "I thought I saw something out of the corner of my eye so I stopped at the dining room. There was a woman in the room just standing there. She wore a black dress with a big skirt—a hoop skirt. I could only see the bottom part of her skirt. I realized that she was walking towards me. I thought, 'I don't really want to be here when she gets to the door to greet me!'"

Although Sophia is the most frequently sighted ghost, Grace Bird Kelton also has a strong presence in the house she loved so well. At one wedding reception there was even a place set for "Grace Kelton, (deceased)" at the Bride's table.

My friend and psychic researcher Anne Oscard told me about her visits to Kelton House:

"As for Grace, oh, she's there all right! I've smelled her perfume and felt cold spots up by the door to her room. She's never particularly bothered me, but the very first time I walked into the place, my initial question was, 'Who's that formidable woman who's half-visible at the front door?' It was Grace.

"I will never forget the time my friend Brian* met Grace. He went to Kelton House with me to help out when I gave a speech. Just before the program, I took him upstairs to show him Grace's room. He kept telling me that he didn't believe in ghosts, that he thought the entire thing was silly, etc. etc. When we got to the top of the stairs, just outside Grace's bedroom, the man gasped and staggered backward.

"'Oh, my God!' he said, then turned and ran down the stairs. I found him out in the garden having a smoke. His hands were shaking and he was sweating.

"'She was there!' he gasped. 'I felt the most terrible cold spot right there on top of me!' It was almost as if she had walked *through* him. I've never seen him so shaken."

Grace seems to have a touch of the autocrat in her makeup. One tour guide had some guests who talked through her entire tour. She took them into the dining room. They stood with their backs against the china cabinet and as they stood there the door of the china cabinet popped out and hit them in the rear. Perhaps this was Grace's way of saying "Oh, be*have!*"

The Chinese character for "discord" shows two women under one roof. Two ghostly ladies squabbling over the deed to Kelton House could get awkward. Yet it does not seem as though Sophia and Grace ever meet. Perhaps each still sees the house as it was in her own day and serenely considers herself the sole mistress of her realm. Two very different women; two very different ghosts. Yet they both cherished this house and that may be why they linger.

Visiting the site

Handicapped access is restricted to the main floor. The Kelton House staff is in the process of developing a video tour of the second floor.

See p. 105 for more Columbus haunt-spots.

Directions

Kelton House Museum & Garden
586 East Town Street
Columbus, OH 43215
(614) 464-2022

From the west, take I-70 East to the Main Street exit, bear right, turn left onto Parsons Ave. at Main and Parsons, then turn left onto Town Street from Parsons. From the east, take I-70 West to I-71 North. Take the Broad Street exit, turn right onto Broad and then an immediate left onto Parsons. Go about three blocks, and turn right onto Town Street. Parking on Town Street is limited; the Kelton House parking lot is on Franklin Ave.

23

THE UNDERTAKER'S REVENGE
Briggs Lawrence County
Public Library
Ironton

We are the hollow men...

-T. S. Eliot-

Ironton was named for its once-vigorous iron smelting industry. In its heyday, it boasted an opera house, five movies theatres and thirteen hotels. Its furnaces blazed profitably until the 1920s. It was then that the forests which supplied the charcoal for the furnaces were depleted. Many furnaces were dismantled and moved to West Virginia. Today Ironton is a pretty little town, but a quiet little town. The dead buried in the local Woodland Cemetery outnumber the living.

Briggs Lawrence County Public Library

Briggs Lawrence County Public Library is built on the site of the house of Dr. Joseph Lowry, whose story is told below.

HAUNT HISTORY

I've always been fascinated by stories of burial alive, of the Golden Age of body-snatching. I think that's why this story is so dear to my heart. In fact, one might say it evokes a truly *visceral* response....

"Well, the key phrase here is 'reputedly haunted,'" Marta Ramey*, Genealogy Librarian of Briggs Lawrence told me when I asked about local reputedly haunted sites. "Some people say that Dr. Lowry, whose house stood on the corner where this library was built walks around it looking for his body parts."

Body parts? Who could resist a ghost story that began so ghoulishly?

The tale started innocently enough with a well-respected local doctor found dead in his bed. Dr. Joseph W. Lowry, age 68, a wealthy physician and active Republican political figure was found dead in his pajamas at his "palatial" home at 321 South Fourth Street on the afternoon of Wednesday, May 24, 1933. His wife, Sarah, had died two years before, in 1931 and he lived alone.

Some patients who had been unable to get in touch with Dr. Lowry had spoken to Mr. Riley, a close friend of the deceased, who climbed through the bedroom window. The door that led from Dr. Lowry's room into the hall was locked. All windows were latched, except the one through which Riley entered. Although the weather had been warm, the heater in the bathroom nearby was turned up full and the house was swelteringly hot.

"Dr. Lowry was found in his bed, his head swathed in a towel, his arms crossed on his chest. One cover covered his body up to the arm pits and another had been pulled down over the foot of the bed. Blood had run down one side of his face from his nose and mouth. A large electric light was burning in the ceiling just over the foot of the bed...."[1]

Originally it was thought that the doctor had a stroke. The towel over his face was explained by the neighbors saying that Dr. Lowry

*My deepest thanks to Marta, who not only "dug up" the newspaper clippings used in this story, but went out of her way to photograph the library and cemetery.

"usually kept lights burning in the residence at night and he probably placed the towel over his face to keep light from his eyes...."[2]

Dr. Lowry's funeral, held at his home, was handled by the Schneider undertakers of Chesapeake and he was laid to rest in his $40,000 mausoleum at Woodland Cemetery next to the bodies of his wife and mother. Although one might reasonably have expected Dr. Lowry to rest in peace, local newspaper headlines tell an increasingly lurid story:

"Dr. J.W. Lowry's Body Found After Entrance Is Forced To His Home, Well Known Physician Had Stroke Tuesday Night"[3]

"Mystery Envelops Lowry Estate, Attorneys Unable to Locate Safety Deposit Box Referred to in Note On Key Left By the Late Physician in Local Box"[4]

"Believed To Have Been Murdered; Examination To Be Held This Afternoon"[5]

"We Know Dr. Lowry Was Murdered, He Was Victim of Friends, Not Enemies," Says Sheriff Bennett "Don't Ask Us to Tell Too Much, It May Give Somebody a Chance to Frame An Alibi."[6]

Official suspicions were first aroused when a key to a safe deposit box was found, but the box could not be located. It was whispered that several of Lowry's strong boxes had been emptied

Lowry Mausoleum

by his sister Alice Barger and nephew Clark, who were said to have borrowed money from Lowry in the past. Worse, on the exhumation morning when the authorities needed a key to the mausoleum, the Bargers were nowhere to be found. Authorities forced an entrance using a torch to burn through the heavy metal doors. To this day they have not been repaired and are chained together.

Dr. Lowry's body was autopsied at the Feuchter & Davison Funeral Home on Tuesday morning. A surprise awaited. The doctor's body was filled with excelsior [wood shavings] and some vital organs like the liver, stomach and spleen were missing.

Sheriff E. W. Bennett and Coroner H. H. Jones quickly located the intestines of Dr. Lowry "buried on the property of Undertaker Schneider of Chesapeake, who had the Lowry funeral in charge, and last Thursday had taken the vital organs of the late physician to Columbus to be examined by chemists."[7]

The rest of the autopsy revealed that brain, heart and kidneys were normal, thus ruling out cerebral hemorrhage, apoplexy, or heart failure. Suspicious red "unnatural" marks, which "stretch across the throat the width of a man's hand"[8] were found on the dead doctor's neck and there was some slight injury to the head behind the left ear. Now the headlines read: "Natural Cause Eliminated in Lowry Case, Officials Lean to Theory of Asphyxiation. May Have Been Partially Stunned and Suffocated."[9]

Dr. Lowry's wealth could certainly have provided a motive for murder. Estimates of his fortune began at $100,000, with the final figure being closer to $300,000. The Bargers were the sole heirs.

Was he murdered? Why were his insides removed? Here we enter into the realm of conjecture. What follows is entirely speculative, based on local hearsay, gossip, and innuendo, sometimes a more reliable source of truth than the most carefully sworn testimony:

The story goes that when Dr. Lowry's wife Sarah died in 1931, he ordered a very expensive, custom-made polished wood coffin. When it arrived, it had a slight scratch. Dr. Lowry noticed it at once. The undertaker murmured that it could easily be repaired. The French polisher could be on the job within the hour....

Dr. Lowry cut him short. It wouldn't do. He wouldn't be imposed upon with shoddy, second-rate goods. He insisted on being shown the coffins in stock and selected one, a top-of-the-line model, to be sure, with the genuine imitation mahogany veneer but a good deal less costly than the custom-made coffin. Dr. Lowry knew perfectly well that the custom coffin could be fixed but perhaps he was having second thoughts about the Dear Departed, or it may have been one of those minor economies that keep the rich richer than you and me.

The undertaker had not insisted on payment when the order was placed. He went home with a splitting headache and his wife put cool cloths on his forehead while he railed against the miserly doctor. He was his usual unctuous professional self by the time he next saw the doctor at the funeral. But he had the coffin taken up into the loft of the carriage house and covered with a horse blanket. On sleepless nights he brooded over the unpaid coffin invoice.

So when the news came that Dr. Lowry was dead, the undertaker danced a little jig of delight. He had sworn that Lowry would go to go his eternal rest in that expensive casket but it had been made for the Doctor's wispy little wife and the dead man's bulging midsection made it impossible to close the lid. Piece of cake, said the undertaker, preening himself on his ingenuity. He simply scooped out the internal organs, shoveled in a few handfuls of excelsior, stitched up the now much-diminished belly, and voila! Not only was the coffin a perfect fit but the old man looked trimmer than he had ever looked in life. The heirs congratulated him on how well the old man looked. Only a few people seemed puzzled by the corpse's diminished height. Oh well, they went away thinking, the dead *always* look smaller... It had been a simple matter to take up the old man's legs a bit so the undertaker could cram him into the coffin crafted for the five-foot Sarah.

Soon, however, rumors began to fly around the town that the old man's death wasn't altogether a natural one. There was some suspicion that someone had helped the old boy along—either by poison or a pillow over the face.

The autopsy revealed a startling secret, but not the one expected. When questioned, the undertaker admitted that he'd taken a few liberties with the old man's innards. Motivated entirely by spite, he said cheerfully. The undertaker led the authorities to the place he'd buried the remains of the Doc, but the parts in question were too far gone to be analyzed for poison. Any possible case against the heirs was dismissed for lack of evidence.[10]

But to return to today and the absolute, literal truth....

Mary, a clerk in the Children's Department, was sitting with Naomi Deer, author of *The History of Woodland Cemetery, Ironton, Ohio*, as well as several relatives and a fellow worker, Jeannette, discussing Dr. Lowry's mysterious end and the stories of his haunting the Library.

"Jeannette didn't believe it," Mary told me. "All of a sudden, the scanner went >beep<. We looked at the computer screen. Normally when you scan a book, the computer will pull up just the name of the patron checking the book out. This screen showed a list of four or five patrons' names—all 'Lowry.'

"OK," I said. And I cleared the screen. All of a sudden the scanner beeped again." This time the screen showed that *The Ghost and Mrs. Muir* had been checked out, even though the book was still downstairs in the stacks.

"OK, Dr. Lowry," Mary said. "it's time to leave me alone."

Mary and other library employees have said that as they are leaving at closing they hear keys jingling. At that everyone gets quiet, clutching their own keys tightly to silence them. And they still hear what sounds like keys rattling. They've checked repeatedly to see that they weren't locking anyone in but there is never anyone there.

Marta told me, "One morning I was in the children's dept. (right down the hall from the room where I work, the Phyllis Hamner Room for Genealogy and Local History) and I heard the door to my room close. This was in the morning before we opened but there were several employees there. The door is hydraulic so it pushes open easily but takes about thirty seconds to close. I went down the hall and opened the door to see if someone needed me. There was nobody in the room. I let the door go shut and went

Means Monument

back to children's. About a minute later I heard the door close again. Upon checking, it was the same. The third time this happened I ran down the hall to inspect and.... no one! I laughed and said. 'Okay, Doc, knock it off.' That was the last time it happened."

Dr. Lowry, along with his mother and his wife, are all buried in Woodland Cemetery in a vaguely Egyptian, deco-style mausoleum. Inside the mausoleum are stained-glass portraits of Joseph, his wife and both their mothers.

The Cemetery contains many interesting and odd monuments and is well worth a

Wilson Monument

visit. One monument is the Means cross, a huge cross of solid stone about twenty feet tall and two feet thick. While the monument was being hoisted into place, it fell onto one of the workers crushing him to death. A man who always took a short cut through the cemetery in darkness on his way to work used to see a ghost loitering by the monument. One night he took his gun with him and shot at the spook. The bullet passed right through the spirit and slammed into the stone. You can still see the bullet hole today.

Then there is the stone of Mrs. Wilson. When alive, she and her husband fought continually. She died from an accidental fall down a flight of stairs. Her statue has a discoloration around her stone neck which appeared as soon as the statue was placed at the site. While her husband was living he had the stone sand blasted several times to try to remove the stains but they would reappear within days. She also has stains on her cheeks that look like tears running down her face.

It is said that Dr. Lowry also roams the cemetery in search of his missing insides. His mother, who died when she was thrown from a carriage by a spooked horse, haunts the cemetery as well. It is said that the pair stroll toward the entrance of the cemetery but never go farther that the bridge that goes over the highway.[11] There are no tales of Dr. Lowry walking out with his wife Sarah. Perhaps there were domestic reasons he had balked at that expensive coffin.

What do mother and son talk of on these phantom promenades? Mrs. Lowry leans on her son's arm, her broken neck nodding gently in agreement with his complaints. Broken legs! Wantonly plundered bowels! As one of the First Citizens of Ironton, he is outraged at his post-mortem manhandling! And that sister of his! Putting extravagant hot-house wreaths (at least for the first few years, while people were watching) up against those expensive mausoleum gates she'd had chained together like old tool shed doors! It would make him sick to his stomach, he declares, if he had any. And so Dr. Lowry and his mother hobble for eternity through Woodland Cemetery. Rest, Dr. Lowry. Rest in pieces.

Visiting the site

The Library is handicapped accessible. For handicapped accessibility, take the driveway beside the library off Fourth Street to the parking lot in back.

Other local haunt-spots:
Woodland Cemetery, 824 Lorain St, Ironton, OH 45638-2841

Directions

Briggs Lawrence County Public Library
321 South Fourth Street
Ironton, Ohio 45638

Web site: http://www.lawrence.lib.oh.us/

From Rt. 52 take the Ironton exit for Rt 93. From the exit make a right toward downtown Ironton. Due to the design of the exits you will make a right whether going east or west on Rt. 52. This will put you on Rt. 93 or Park Ave. Go to Fifth Street and make a left onto Fifth. Take the second right, which is Washington. The library is on your right at the corner of 4th and Washington.

To get to Woodland Cemetery: From Rt. 52 take the Coal Grove exit (Rt. 243). If you are going east, make a left from the exit; if going west, take a right turn. After the ramps back to Rt. 52, take the first left turn, Carlton Davidson Lane. Follow this street to the Cemetery.

24

BLESSED ARE THE POOR IN SPIRIT
The Wood County Historical Center
Bowling Green

'Are there no prisons?' asked Scrooge.

'Plenty of prisons,' said the gentleman, laying down the pen again.

'And the Union workhouses?' demanded Scrooge. 'Are they still in operation?'

'They are. Still,' returned the gentleman, 'I wish I could say they were not.'

'Under the impression that they scarcely furnish Christian cheer of mind or body to the multitude,' returned the gentleman, 'a few of us are endeavouring to raise a fund to buy the Poor some meat and drink. and means of warmth. We choose this time, because it is a time, of all others, when Want is keenly felt, and Abundance rejoices. What shall I put you down for?'

'Nothing!' Scrooge replied.

'You wish to be anonymous?'

'I wish to be left alone,' said Scrooge. 'Since you ask me what I wish, gentlemen, that is my answer. I don't make merry myself at Christmas and I can't afford to make idle people merry. I help to support the establishments I have mentioned — they cost enough; and those who are badly off must go there.'

'Many can't go there; and many would rather die.'

'If they would rather die,' said Scrooge, 'they had better do it, and decrease the surplus population

-Charles Dickens, *"A Christmas Carol"* *(1843)*-

Built in 1868, for 102 years this building served as the county poor farm, also called "The Wood County Infirmary" or "The Wood County Home." It housed the county's orphans and unwed mothers, the sick and homeless, paupers and the handicapped, the elderly and the insane. The harsh credo of the Home was "to keep the genuinely needy from starving without breeding a class of paupers who choose to live off public bounty rather than to work." If you were poor or in dire straits, the bureaucrats proclaimed self-righteously, it was not because of bad luck or family problems, it was because you were lazy and didn't practice Industry and Thrift.

The Home was a place of last resort. Imagine that you have worked hard all your life, that you have managed to scrape together some land and a house for your wife and six children. Then disaster strikes with the lightning that burns down your barn with half of your livestock. Your eldest son dies of meningitis and you mangle your arm so badly in a threshing machine that it has to be cut off. The bank forecloses. No one will hire a man with one arm. There is no welfare, no Social Security. So rather than starve your wife and remaining children to death, you take what little you still possess and go to the Home. There you and the two boys are sent to the men's dormitory in the East Wing. Your wife and the babies are sent to the Women's Wing. You will see each other in passing as you go about your work but you will eat and sleep in separate rooms. You have heard of other unfortunates who got back on their feet again and were able to leave the Home. You hope you will be one of them.

The building is shaped like a giant "U." The "West Wing" of the building housed the superintendent and matron, a husband-and-wife team, along with their staff. Inmates were seldom allowed in

Wood County Historical Center and Museum
and part of "The Brandeberry Wall"

the West Wing. The middle of the "U" was the Center or Woman's Wing while the East Wing quartered the men and boys.

Originally the facility stood on 200 acres and was nearly self-sufficient. If they could work, inmates were expected to help with farm chores. They grew their own food and raised livestock. The Home's cattle barn was the largest in the county until the night it burned in 1965. Ice was harvested from the ice ponds and stored in the enormous icehouse, providing year-round refrigerated storage. The property contained its own hospital, gas wells, cemetery, and mental asylum—the "Lunatic House," nicknamed "Jail," where the violent mentally-ill patients raved behind bars. The attics and basements of the Men's and Women's Wings were also used to house "unsound" people. There were no drugs or therapies for mental illness in those days. "Lunatics," who could encompass the mentally retarded, the schizophrenic, or the depressed, could only be locked up.

An inspection in 1878 found the institution to be "not in generally good order." Shortly afterwards, Edwin Farmer and his wife Charlotte took over and made the Home a model institution. It even had its own supply of natural gas from the two wells on the property. Frank Brandeberry and his wife Lottie, daughter of Charlotte and Edwin, succeeded the Farmers and served as superintendent and matron until 1959. It was Frank who, in 1920, designed and, with inmate help, built the stone and cement wall and the cement picket fence—"The Brandeberry Wall"—a special point of pride for the Historical Center. By all accounts Mr. Farmer and Mr. Brandeberry were enlightened and humane administrators who did their best to see that the inmates were well treated.

Normally there might have been some sixty inmates. In the dark days of the Depression, 144 people lived here. In 1971 the facility was closed and was slated for demolition. In 1972, Lyle Fletcher, secretary of the Park Commission and editor and archivist of the Wood County Historical Society, fought against tearing the building down. Backed by many in the community, he argued that the building should be turned over to the Wood County Historical Society for use as a museum. The Museum opened for public tours in the spring of 1975.[1] The Wood County Historical Center now houses a fascinating and eclectic mix of exhibits covering the whole spectrum of Wood County history.

Only a few artifacts survive from the original Home but here you can find just about anything else: a ringneck pheasant shot by actor Clark Gable in 1935 when he visited Wood County; a Civil War-era amputation kit, gleaming in its red plush-lined case; a space-age design electric stove bought at the 1939 World's Fair; and a coverlet made from county fair hog show ribbons.

Special events, tours and re-enactments keep history alive at the Museum. A Halloween Folklore and Fun Fest held in October includes a tour on which you can hear some of the stories the staff so generously shared with me. As Anne Touvell, Assistant to the Director says, "We're Wood County's best-kept secret!"

HAUNT HISTORY

It was a dark and rainy day in May when I visited the Museum with my friend Linda. Even in the rain, the white-painted porches of the building and the stone-and-cement arches gave the property a gala, Fourth-of-July air. I expected to see bunting hung from the porches and people in their summer clothes sipping lemonade. The reality was fascinating but alas, much less festive.

Anne Touvell, standing at the front entryway, gave us an introductory talk about the history of the Home. It was on the path leading to this porch that a mysterious black-cloaked figure was seen by a Museum worker in 1999. She had been working late at night in her office and, glancing out her window, saw what looked like a man in a black cape coming up the path to the front door. Glancing at her watch, she saw that it was 10:30 p.m., much too late for visitors. When she looked up again, the man was gone. Even later, as she was locking up, she again saw the man in the dark cloak striding up the path to the front door, in exactly the same place she had seen him before. He got to within a few yards of the door—then disappeared.[2]

After Anne's introduction, Linda and I took the self-guided tour. Each room was labeled with its original purpose: Superintendent's Office, Hired Girl's Bedroom, Men's Dining Room. We wandered from the parlor with its handsome antique furniture to the hallway display of a Civil War Union uniform worn by a local soldier, then we climbed the stairs to the second-floor West Wing hallway, the site of a mysterious occurrence in the late 1980s. A worker was busy with sanding the hall floor, then varnishing it. Each night he would close the windows, only to find one window open in one of the bedrooms upstairs in the West Wing the next morning. He began to feel as if he was not alone. Finally the nagging feeling of being watched made him turn. He saw an old woman, smiling at him. Then, she disappeared. Not spooking easily, he carried on varnishing the floor. When he came in the next morning, there were two small footprints in the middle of the gleaming floor—coming and going to nowhere.[3]

The further away from the West Wing we went, the colder it got. We worked our way around to the Center Wing where the women's dining room had been. It is now divided into three rooms holding children's, laundry and kitchen exhibits. The children's exhibit displayed toys and games that, ironically, few of the inmate's children could have afforded. At the threshold of the laundry exhibit room I was hit on the back of the neck. I saw two women flailing at each other, fighting in what was then the dining room.

The Weston Room is the first room in the East Wing. Mr. Dorsey Sergent, a Bowling Green pharmacist, filled prescriptions for the Home in the 1960s. Since there were often many bottles of medicine to be sorted and filled, it was after 3 a.m. one night when Sergent and his co-worker arrived at the darkened building. They let themselves in through the front door, then walked in the dark through the old dining room and towards the nurses' station in the East Wing. The only light was the moon shining through the windows.

The two pharmacists were startled by the figure of an elderly woman in a white nightgown and night cap stepping into the hallway before them. "Where did *she* come from?" they thought. The woman smiled at them as they passed. They turned around and she was gone—dissolved into moonlight.

Shaken, the men rushed to the nurses' station. "Who was that lady in the hall who scared the dickens out of us?" they demanded.

The nurse had no idea what they were talking about.

"There's no one in the rooms you just walked through," she said. And to make sure, they searched the rooms but could find no trace of the old woman in white. The little old lady in white is known as "Agnes." She has been seen many times wandering all over the Museum.[4]

I was still rubbing my neck as we viewed the school pictures in the Alumni Room. This room houses old yearbooks, graduation programs, baseballs, and pennants. It ought to be a place of pleasant reminiscence. Instead, it was a dark room with a lingering memory of cruelty hanging over it. Suddenly I heard a howl. I was struck by a sickening fear I could almost smell. Then I heard the thud of fists on flesh.

In the hall beyond the Alumni Room, I slumped into an old church pew for a moment of quiet. It was perishingly cold. Opposite me sat an old wheelchair which, the sign said, had originally been in the Home. The wheelchair was small and delicate, its back a sunburst of spindles. In it sat an old woman, nodding a tremulous head, smiling and drooling. I could see a white strip of cloth just beneath her breasts, knotted to the chair, holding her upright.

Next was the Government Memorial Room, with a wall devoted to the Wood County Crime Collection. Not for the faint of heart, the exhibits were both appalling and riveting. Here you can see the corn cutter Carl Bach used to hack his wife Mary to death in 1881. You can also see Mary Bach's desiccated fingertips preserved in a jar. Further along in the case is a knife taken from an "insane man" on Oregon Road in March of 1950; also the gun used by Arthur Peebles to kill Eugene A. Roth. Next to the gun is the shirt worn by Mr. Roth on that fatal occasion, with a helpful label: "note bloodstain and bullet hole on the right." Other exhibits show a dental cream tube packed with six hacksaw blades, smuggled into some hopeful prisoner who hoped to saw his way to freedom, a Crocodile Dundee-sized bowie knife, and souvenir portraits of "those electrocuted at Columbus." It is Wood County's own Chamber of Horrors.

Leaving Linda lingering by the noose that ended Carl Bach's life, I moved upstairs to the women's sitting room. There I found a group photo of elderly ladies sitting in the bare-walled room—their hair pinned up in buns, their clothing, worn cotton calicos. One ghostly woman had rocked back and forth while the camera did its slow work, leaving a spooky trail of images. I wandered through the sitting room, looking at the miniature models of the icehouse, the pest house, where contagious inmates were segregated, and the cattle barn. I turned to catch a brief glimpse of a woman looking out the window. "I beg your pardon," I said without thinking. There was no one there, of course.

The rooms off the women's sitting room were arranged as mini-museums: one on military history, one on transportation, one on education. In the military room, I blinked and the room was suddenly a bare room furnished only with two beds and a washstand. In a blink, the room was again full of uniforms and flags.

One of the creepiest rooms contained quotes, photographs and life stories of some of the inmates. An original bed from the Home gave off a deeply disturbing atmosphere. I attributed my fear to the horror stories I was reading: grim sagas of neglect, misery and of the routine unthinking cruelties of society. It was only afterwards that Linda told me that room had been used as a morgue.

I was drawn to a photo of "Bert," whose one leg was much shorter than the other. He was an inmate here in the 1930s and 40s. He stares into the sun with a broad, goofily disturbing smile, posing proudly with the little red wagon that he dragged everywhere. Bert was a gentle-spirited fixture of the Home, in death as in life. Many visitors have seen him pulling his ghostly little red wagon around the grounds, have felt him brush by them, or have heard him singing hymns to himself. The fascinating thing is, visitors to the Museum reported seeing his distinctive figure *before* his photo was discovered and put on display.[5]

After we finished our walking tour, Linda and I went downstairs and found Anne in her office. She graciously took us on a complete tour of places not normally open to the public, staying well past closing to make sure we saw everything.

The first stop was the third floor of the West Wing, at one time the women's attic dorm, which is now a storage facility. The sign explained that "noisy, disagreeable inmates were put in the dorm, while agreeable ones were given rooms."

The attic was full of tall rows of shelves. Curator Carole Spencer said, "I was working up here on a three-step stepladder. Well, I took a wrong step and stepped off into nothing and I swear—someone caught me from behind! I was on the way down—right off the ladder. There was *no* way I could have righted myself. I felt hands, one on my shoulder, the other on my rib cage. I came downstairs and found everybody there and accounted for. I didn't even say anything about it for a few days. I just thought, 'Somebody's looking out for me.' And believe me I say 'Thank you,' all the time!"

While Carole feels generally positive impressions in the women's attic, she says "the attic of the Men's Wing—it's tenser, not as comfortable. Maybe that's because it's damp and not in as good a physical condition."

There are *lots* of cold spots, something you'd expect in a drafty old building but "They change," Carole says. "You get the feeling that somebody's watching you. I *hear* more than see things. You can hear people talking and I'll think that there is somebody in the women's sitting room. Nobody. I can't really pick up words, just voices, and it *could* be an echo from people talking downstairs."

I cautiously leaned into one of the many little windowless rooms or closets under the eaves in the attic. There was an echo of the sound of someone pounding on the slanted roof with his fists, sobbing, and a slobbery cry, "Don't hurt me!" I flinched back. Later Carole told me that a dark-colored KKK robe is stored in that closet. She added that it gave off some *very* negative impressions.

Still in the attic storage area, I paced up the outer aisle past baby carriages, shelves of glassware and past a coffin reeking of formaldehyde only I could smell, wrapped in an avocado-green striped sheet. The sobbing of the phantom boy in the closet was gut-wrenching. I wanted to shriek and beat the doors down. I got tenser and tenser, stabbing at the paper as I took my notes. It felt like my head was going to explode. I caught a glimpse of military uniforms on racks under sheets and scurried beyond them. Linda, following behind me, gestured at the uniforms.

"That explains it," she said. Perhaps I was picking up the terrible feelings of aggression and madness from the uniforms. Perhaps not.

Anne opened the door to the center attic. "For me the dividing line is this fire door—you step through there, you step through to the other side," she said. And soon, I saw what she meant. The center attic was dark, with a dusty floor. Christmas trees stood shrouded in black garbage bags in one corner. I wanted to swirl and swoop and dance madly in the ballroom-size space. Then I was drawn to another closet, this one with a chimney running up one wall. At the far end, crouching down to make himself as small as possible, was the ghost of a mentally retarded man. He had his hands cocked in front of him like a kangaroo, and he was snuffling wretchedly. The air was getting colder and colder.

Another door took us through to the East Wing attic, which was formerly the men's dorm. There was a metal dress form, as skeletal as a starved woman in a chicken-wire skirt, a spidery spool-legged table and an atrocious feeling of shame in one corner. The room was crowded with artifacts—filing cabinets, a poster of Clark Gable, baskets, crocks—and another wailing ghost in the closet. Still another ghost pawed at me as I completed the circuit of the room. We retraced our steps and returned to the West Wing attic, the storage room. It was like being back in the land of the living.

"Would you like to see the Lunatic House?" Anne asked cheerily. As we crossed the lush green of the grounds, some childlike spirit hiding under the verandah peered up as we walked by. Anne unlocked the Lunatic House door and I went in by myself, leaving Linda and Anne outside. I cringed through room after room of peeling paint, past assorted artifacts: an old telephone switchboard, an iron lung horribly like a coffin and empty beds.

The silence was broken only by long-silent screaming. In a back room, a phantom attendant was wrestling with a woman in a sack— actually a dirty white armless dress, draw-stringed at the ankles allowing the inmate to move only with tiny unbalanced steps. The crazed paint on the walls seemed to form a road map to the land of the insane.

To my horror, I began to see the room through nineteenth-century lunatic eyes. I was no longer just an observer but an inmate. Here, the paint began to bubble and seethe. There, the floor fell away beneath my feet. Here was a fresh stain on the floor that had been scrubbed away years ago. In a room with a barred window, the rumpled bed tick still bore the impress of a body. The bath had a pit toilet and a tile floor with a drain. I felt the slap of cold water hitting mad flesh and shuddered.

"As long as I don't touch anything," I thought desperately, "I'll be all right."

I dragged myself up the stairs to the second floor. From the hall, I heard someone long dead, crying "I want my mommy!" In a small room off a bathroom, its toilet choked with rust, a ghostly woman with cropped hair crouched, showing her toothless gums in a soundless yowl. In a room at the end of the hall, I heard gibbering at the window; a ghostly inmate was looking over at the verandah of the main building, chanting, singsong: "fil-thy, fil-thy, fil-thy."

Then, there was a kind of unnatural peace until I got to the top of the stairs. I started down them unsteadily, only to find the way blocked by the ghost of a huge and powerful man hurling himself back and forth with the mad strength of the psychotic. He smashed his body first into the banister then into the wall. Bashing this way; crashing that, until I expected the wood to splinter. The attendants

The "Lunatic House"

struggled with him, forcing him down the stairs. He was in front of me, behind me—he *was* me. I made small squeaking noises of distress, trying not to attract the attention of those outside, then I was back in the twenty-first century, in the cool green air.

While Linda went into the building, I methodically studied the plaque on the outside of the Lunatic House. Built in 1884-85 to house the violent mentally ill inmates, it had cells, hospital rooms on the second floor, a bath, and a room for the attendants. I read it over and over, not absorbing a single word. Anne confirmed that inmates were hosed down in the tile-floored bathroom. We walked back to the main building.

There I asked Director Stacey Hann-Ruff if she had had any ghostly experiences. "I'm immune!" she said with a smile. She pondered the changes coming to the Museum. There are 160+ windows. Half have been replaced and it is necessary to replace the other half to continue to control the environment and to safeguard the artifacts.

"What I regret is that all the windows and doors will be replaced and when that happens, we won't have some of the interesting noises and other things happening. The wind used to blow through the attic and the door wouldn't stay shut! It would open and shut, open and shut!"

Anne spoke next. "I try to be rational," she said "One afternoon I was in my office. Stacey went out—I thought. A few minutes later, I heard her come back in and heard papers rustling on her desk. When I didn't hear her go out again, I looked into her office. There was nobody there."

Anne continued, "The other day it was pretty lively around here. *Everybody* was feeling stuff. From five to seven-thirty, it was especially active. There were footsteps everywhere. This always happens when the weather's about to change. The building just sort of gets nervous. I called my roommate and turned up the music. I figure, 'They're doing their thing and that's fine. I just don't want to hear it!'"

Afterwards Linda and I wandered in the rain through the pauper cemetery, where Wood County's poor and unidentified dead were laid to rest under tombstones identical save for a single engraved number. The rain was coming down harder as we walked back to the parking lot.

The Museum's dark windows were suddenly watchful. The ghosts of too many "unsound" people are still here. Lacking a link to reality in life, they still wander the only home they ever knew. Death has not restored them to health or sanity. The administrators did their best to treat the inmates with kindness. And it is a fascinating museum! But there is an inherent melancholy in the building. The Home was the end of the line for many of those who came here. I think that even the poorest and the maddest inmates knew it.

Driving back to my own home and family, I brooded on the experience of being inside the skin of a nineteenth-century lunatic. It was a horrifying place to visit and not a place I'd want to live. And I pondered those words of Christ, so often used to justify harsh treatment of the destitute. "The poor are always with you."

Visiting the site

NOTE: The Lunatic House is currently under renovation and will reopen when work is completed. The attics are not open to the public.

There is a handicapped entrance to the side of the main entrance. Only the ground floor is accessible. There are many stairs and no elevators.

Wood County pauper cemetery

I like to have lunch at Sam B's, 146 N. Main St., Bowling Green, OH 43402-2418, (419) 353-2277. Two other good restaurants in Bowling Green are Call of the Canyon Café, 109 N. Main St., Bowling Green, OH 43402-2419, (419) 353-2255, and Easy Street Café, 104 S. Main St., Bowling Green, OH 43402-2909, (419) 353-0988. Calico, Sage, & Thyme, 115 Clay St., Bowling Green, OH 43402-2309, (419) 352-5417, is a charming local gift shop. If your tastes run to antiques, there are also several antique malls in downtown Bowling Green, and the huge Jeffrey's Antique Gallery 20 miles down the road at the exit for Twp. Road 99. You'll see it on the right from I-75; it's very hard to miss.

Another local haunt-spot is Bowling Green State University's Joe E. Brown and Eva Marie Saint Theatres (*Haunted Ohio*, p. 51; *Haunted Ohio IV*, p. 99)

Directions

The Wood County Historical Center/Museum
13660 County Home Road
Bowling Green, OH 43402
(419) 352-0967

Web site: http://wcnet.org/~wchisctr/

Three miles southeast of Bowling Green, on County Home Road, 1/4 mile east of the I-75/ US Route 6 interchange. Exit #179 off I-75.

APPENDIX 1

BRING OUT YOUR DEAD:
Ohio's Ghostly Tours

These are serious tours, focusing on the history and haunts of a site, *not* commercial "haunted house" attractions. Don't expect burly spirits in hockey masks to leap out of bushes with bloody chainsaws. If you write for information, please enclose a stamped, self-addressed envelope. Many of these tours are run by volunteers at local historical societies and their funds are limited. For more tours throughout the US and beyond, see www.invink.com/helpful.html.

NAME: **[CINCINNATI] HAUNTED CINCINNATI TOUR**
LOCATION: Cincinnati, OH
DESCRIPTION: Sites like Eden Park, Music Hall, Resor House and some sites in northern Kentucky, including Bobby Mackey's Music World. The sites vary from year to year.
TIME: Held once a year, the October Saturday just before Halloween. The tour lasts approximately half a day: 9 a.m.-12 noon.
FEE: Yes
HANDICAPPED ACCESSIBLE: No. This is a bus tour that takes visitors to various private homes and public places. There are many steps in some of the sites visited.
CONTACT INFORMATION: Cincinnati Museum Center's Heritage Program, (513) 287-7031 for reservations.

NAME: **[CLERMONT CO.] TOURS OF HAUNTED HISTORICAL CLERMONT COUNTY**
LOCATION: Various locations throughout Clermont County
DESCRIPTION: A bus tour of approximately 3 or 4 places throughout the county. Past sites have included Spate House, the Wattle House, Promont, and Smyrna Cemetery.
TIME: Approximately 4 hours. Always in the dark!
FEE: Yes
HANDICAPPED ACCESSIBLE: No
CONTACT INFORMATION: Richard Crawford, (513) 724-6222. The October tours fill up quickly but you can book a private tour.

NAME: **[CLEVELAND] NORTH COAST GHOST TOURS**
LOCATION: Cleveland, OH
DESCRIPTION: A bus tour of approximately ten haunted Cleveland-area sites, like Grays Armory and local cemeteries. Sites vary from year to year.
TIME: Approximately 3 hours, although a longer, 5-hour tour is also available.
FEE: Yes
HANDICAPPED ACCESSIBLE: No
CONTACT INFORMATION: Barb Zamlin, 2776 Benjamin Dr, Brunswick, OH 44212, (330) 225-1519 Reservations required.

NAME: **[COLUMBUS] COLUMBUS LANDMARKS FOUNDATION GHOST TOUR**
LOCATION: Columbus, OH
DESCRIPTION: Sites like Thurber House, Kelton House, Kappa Kappa Gamma Heritage Museum, Topiary Garden and O'Shaughnessy Funeral Home. Sites do vary from year to year.
TIME: Approximately 3 hours
FEE: Yes
HANDICAPPED ACCESSIBLE: This is a walking tour; most of the sites are handicapped accessible. Call for detailed information.
CONTACT INFORMATION: Columbus Landmarks Foundation (614) 221-0227

NAME: **[PERRYSBURG] GARRISON GHOST WALK**
LOCATION: Fort Meigs State Memorial Park, 29100 West River Rd, Perrysburg, OH 43551.
DESCRIPTION: Tours of the haunted Fort Meigs grounds in October.
TIME: Approximately 1 hour
FEE: Yes
HANDICAPPED ACCESSIBLE: No. The tour is a 1-mile walk.
CONTACT INFORMATION: Reservations required. Call (419) 874-4121.

NAME: **[WARREN] WARREN GHOST WALK**
LOCATION: Warren, OH
DESCRIPTION: This walking tour makes approximately seven stops at historic homes located along Millionaires' Row, where actors tell the eerie tales of people who once lived and/or died in Trumbull County.
TIME: Approximately 1 hour
FEE: Yes, discount for advance purchase
HANDICAPPED ACCESSIBLE: The sidewalks are still the original slate in most areas and therefore they are uneven but passable in a wheelchair. The Council is willing to provide an ASL interpreter with advance notice.

Generally they limit the signed tours to one specific day.
CONTACT INFORMATION: Fine Arts Council of Trumbull County, 256
Mahoning Ave, Warren, OH 44483, (330) 399-1212, Web site:
www.trumbullarts.org

NAME: [WAYNESVILLE] NOT SO DEARLY DEPARTED TOUR
LOCATION: Waynesville, OH
DESCRIPTION: This walking tour of "Ohio's most haunted town" includes
13 sites like the Stetson House, Hammel House, and Angel of the Garden
Tea Room
TIME: Approximately 1-1.5 hours
FEE: Yes
HANDICAPPED ACCESSIBLE: Yes. This is a walking tour. The town's
streets have curb cut-outs and participants do not enter the properties.
CONTACT INFORMATION: Waynesville Area Chamber of Commerce (513)
897-8855 or Dennis Dalton, Historically Speaking, (513) 932-5298. Web site:
www.waynesvilleohio.com. Visit the web site for news of special Halloween festivals and tours.

NAME: [ZOAR] LANTERN TOUR OF THE GHOSTS OF ZOAR
LOCATION: Zoar, OH
DESCRIPTION: Hear the accounts of Zoar's resident spirits on a haunted
stroll through the streets of historic Zoar Village by candlelight. Friday and
Saturday nights by reservation only. The times may vary, depending on the
time of year.
TIME: Approximately 45 minutes to 1 hour
FEE: Yes
HANDICAPPED ACCESSIBLE: Only partially. Although participants do not
enter the houses, the streets do not have curb cut-outs. However, it is
possible to lift wheelchairs on and off the curb.
CONTACT INFORMATION: (330) 874-2002 Web site: www.haunted-
ohio.com
NOTE: Despite the web site name, this tour is not associated with my
Haunted Ohio books in any way.

If you know of any tours I have missed, please let me know at
Kestrel Publications, 1811 Stonewood Drive, Dayton, OH 45432-4002,
invisiblei@aol.com. Thanks!

APPENDIX 2

WILD-GHOST CHASE:
How To Hunt Ghosts

The ghosts you chase, you never catch.

-John Malkovich-

How to Hunt Ghosts

My advice to the person who wants to investigate ghostly phe-
nomena is to ask yourself WHY do I want to do this? Is it mere
curiosity? Genuine scientific inquiry? Thrill-seeking? I've talked to
people who were practically salivating at the thought of "stirring up"
something ghostly, for no good reason. They just wanted some
excitement. We all know curiosity killed the cat so if you genuinely
want to investigate ghosts, keep the ouija board in the box, the
candles in the cupboard and your unhealthy curiosity at home. I see
a lot of people who tell themselves "I'm sensitive. I think I'll go
investigate ghosts." That's not enough. You need mental toughness, a
huge amount of common sense—and a certain "sixth sense" as to
when people are putting you on. *First rule of ghost hunting:* Don't be
gullible. *Second rule:* Don't be gullible. *Third rule:* Don't be gullible.

Some other suggestions:

1) Always look at the most natural explanation first, usually it is
the correct one. A woman once wrote to me telling me that the
bathrooms at Disney World were haunted. Her reason? The toilets
flushed by themselves and the water at the sinks turned on mysteriously! She didn't realize that the toilets and sinks were motion-
activated. Remember, your senses will deceive you. I once thought I
saw the glowing tombstone of Woodland Cemetery in Dayton
(*Haunted Ohio III*, p. 49). Instead it was lights over on Brown Street
outlined by some strategically placed tree branches. Ghosts have
been unmasked as white cows in cemeteries, ball lightning, swamp gas,
squirrels in the attic, and Scrooge's famous undigested bit of beef.

2) Never go ghost hunting after dark. Ghosts are just as visible
and numerous in the daytime.

3) Never visit abandoned buildings or trespass on someone else's
property.

4) Never let anyone tell you what is going on in her house if you intend to visit. I try very hard to not know any stories about the site so I can see for myself. If I also experience the same things, then that's evidence, if only circumstantial evidence.

5) Just because someone tells you something happened to him doesn't make it so. I once had a young man call me with a plausible story about a haunted library where he had worked. Then he started on a tale of a haunted school that could have been written by Stephen King, complete with evil entities, disembodied red eyes and rasping demonic voices. I thanked him for calling but emphasized that I would need to talk to the other witnesses. I'm still waiting. People who are making things up usually go a little too far. They may want to be paid, may want publicity, or they may simply want attention.

6) Question witnesses separately. Get them to write out statements before they've had a chance to get their stories straight.

7) Record or write down everything as soon as possible, no matter how silly or insignificant it might seem at the time.

8) Don't use ouija boards, other types of "talking boards" or automatic writing. The material gotten through them is usually valueless and you attract the wrong kind of spirits: lying troublemakers who are just hanging around waiting to cause trouble. They'll impersonate your grandmother or tell you things that later come true just to make you think it's all real. Read Joe Fisher's book, *Hungry Ghosts*. It is the perfect book for anyone who has been impressed by seance or ouija communications.

9) Read everything on the supernatural you can, except for information on demons or black magic. Look at the list of books under "Reference" on my website at www.invink.com. Ask your librarian to order them for you through interlibrary loan. My favorite books about ghosthunting are *How to Find a Ghost* by James Deem (for young adults) and *Ghosts and How to See Them* by Peter Underwood. Visit Deem's website at http://www.jamesmdeem.com. A good place to study ghost books is The Popular Culture Library at Bowling Green State University, which houses the Invisible Ink Collection of true ghost stories. See http://www.bgsu.edu/colleges/library/pcl/pcl24.html for more information.

10) You need to know a little bit about a lot of subjects because you never know when some bit of off-beat knowledge will come in handy. For example, a woman had experienced some minor poltergeist activity, two of her dogs had died suddenly and her boyfriend

was having blinding headaches. The house didn't seem to be haunted but there was something about it that didn't look quite right. She told me that paneling, insulation, and carpeting had been replaced after a major fire. I suspected that something like formaldehyde was leaking out of the new insulation, sickening the boyfriend and the dogs. I suggested that she call the Environmental Protection Agency.

A couple asked me about a strange clicking noise their antique cupboard was making. I assumed it was a beetle infestation, not a ghost. They needed an exterminator rather than an exorcist.

A working knowledge of psychology and medicine is also appropriate since I find many of my "cases" revolve around someone who has personal problems or psychological difficulties using the supernatural as an excuse for not facing up to those problems.

A woman described to me poltergeist-type activities at her home. It turned out that a) she was afraid of a violent soon-to-be-ex-husband and b) she had moved a new boyfriend into her house, enraging the jealous husband further. Talk about stress! It's possible that there was a ghost at her house but given her description of events, it is more likely that she just wanted something else to focus on, so she didn't have to think about her potentially deadly situation.

11) Don't do demons. People who come to you with possession stories are inevitably extremely troubled and they may drag you down with them. Don't be too helpful; people take advantage.

12) Try to always double-check your facts. I heard a story about a house where four young children were killed by their father. Their ghosts supposedly wrote their names behind a bedroom door in crayon. When I read newspaper articles about the tragedy I found that: 1) They didn't die at that house, but at the next place they lived and 2) The names written on the wall were not the dead children's names. Another perfectly good ghost story destroyed by the facts! And understand, you can't PROVE a thing. Your goal should be to record events. Be skeptical but in the best, Fortean sense, not the skepticism of the folks who say, "This couldn't *possibly* happen; therefore, it *didn't*."

I'm often asked how to trace a house's owners/history. Ask your reference librarian about this book on researching your house's history: *House Histories: a guide to tracing the genealogy of your home*, Sally Light, Spencertown, NY: Golden Hill Press, 1989.

I asked my friend and fellow ghost hunter Anne Oscard if she had any ghosthunting advice. She replied:

"My advice to spook stalkers would be: 1) Do not use your imagination, this is how you get into trouble and prove you're an amateur; 2) Prepare to be frustrated most of the time, because under every sheet there does not lurk a ghost; 3) Be as scientific and logical as possible. Take a camera, a tape recorder, and take notes You're looking for serious evidence of a ghostly presence, so take your mission seriously; 4) Do not telephone professional ghost hunters and ask if you can 'hang out' with them sometime. If you're asked along on a ghost hunt, accept it as a compliment. Otherwise, let these people alone. Would you ask a police officer if you could 'hang out' while he makes his rounds, or would you ask a doctor if you could 'hang out' while she performs an operation? If not, then what makes you think a professional ghost hunter might want you in the way?"

Personally I don't use any ghost-hunting devices in my work. I'm sensitive to seeing and sensing ghosts and I am reluctant to use any machine that might cause me to be more dependent on it than on my senses. James Deem recommends these tools: Notebook and pen for taking notes; tape measure and graph paper for plotting location of sensations/sightings; hammer and nails, thread and rubber cement for making sure nothing human can get through a doorway; flour or powder for detecting footprints. Ghosts generally will not leave footprints, but humans will. Always get permission before nailing, sticking or scattering anything! Large weather thermometer for checking changes in temperature. Flashlight, tape recorder, camera and tripod, and extra batteries. Don't rely entirely upon tape recorders, which have a way of failing. Take pen-and-paper notes as well.

A list of the equipment used by ghost hunter Nick Reiter is posted at http://www.alliancelink.com/users/avalon/tools.htm. There is also a great questionnaire on the Avalon Site regarding paranormal experiences. I am no longer visiting private houses but The Avalon Foundation will consider your case.

To recap: don't be led by mere foolish curiosity into visiting graveyards after dark, breaking into abandoned houses or spending the night on railroad tracks looking for spook lights. If you're going to investigate ghosts, you need to make sure your feet are firmly planted in the world of the living. You can enjoy reading about ghosts, visiting haunted sites that are open to the public, and studying the paranormal. But if you are lost in some ghostly fantasyland, you have no business trying to "call up" spirits and no claim to be able to investigate them in any kind of objective way.

APPENDIX 3

Haunted Sites You May Visit In Ohio

These are sites not listed in this book.

ASHTABULA CO.
Ashtabula County District Library, 335 W. 44th St, Ashtabula, OH 44004 (440) 977-9341

AUGLAIZE CO.
Ft. Amanda, 22783 St Rt. 198, Cridersville, OH 45806

BROWN CO.
Baird House, 201 N. 2nd St, Ripley, OH 45167 (937) 392-4918

BUTLER CO.
Miami University, Oxford, OH 45056 Fisher Hall has been torn down, but Marcum Hall and Wilson Hall still stand. (513) 529-1809

CLERMONT CO.
Chateau Laroche, Loveland, OH, (513) 683-4686 Tours or directions
Smyrna Cemetery, Smyrna Rd, 1/2 mile east of Felicity

COLUMBIANA CO.
Beaver Creek State Park, East Liverpool, OH (330) 385-3091

CUYAHOGA CO.
Baldwin-Wallace College, 275 Eastland Road, Berea, OH 44017-2088 (440) 826-2900
Federal Reserve Bank of Cleveland, East 6th and Superior Ave, Cleveland, OH
Squire's Castle, North Chagrin Reserve near Cleveland

ERIE CO.
Cedar Point Amusement Park, 1 Causeway Drive, Sandusky, OH 44870 (419) 626-2350
Merry Go Round Museum, W. Washington and Jackson St., Sandusky, OH (419) 626-6111
Thomas Edison Birthplace, Thomas Edison Birthplace Museum, 9 North Edison Dr., Milan, OH, (419) 499-2135

FRANKLIN CO.
Camp Chase Confederate Cemetery, 2800 block of Sullivant Ave. at Chestershire Rd. and Sullivant.
The Clock Restaurant, 161 N. High St, Columbus, OH 43415 (614) 221-2562
Otterbein College, Cowan Hall, Westerville, OH 43081 (614) 890-0004
Ohio Dominican College, Sansbury Hall, Columbus, OH 43219 (614) 251-4505
The Palace Theatre 34 W. Broad St., Columbus, OH (614) 469-1331
Schmidt's Sausage House, 240 E. Kossuth St., Columbus, OH (614) 444-6808
Worthington Inn, 649 High St, Worthington, OH 43085 (614) 885-7700

GALLIA CO.
Our House Museum, 432 First Ave, Gallipolis, OH 45631 (614) 446-0586

GREENE CO.
Blue Jacket, 520 S Stringtown Rd., Xenia, OH 45385 (937) 376-4318 box office
Eden Hall, 235 E. Second St, Xenia, OH 45485 (937) 376-1274
Magee Park, Little Sugar Creek Road north of 725, Bellbrook, OH
Olde Trail Tavern, 228 Xenia Avenue, Yellow Springs, OH 45387 (937) 767-7448
Sugar Creek Reserve, 7636 Wilmington Pike, Dayton, OH

HAMILTON CO.
Cary Cottage, Clovernook Center for Opportunities, 7000 Hamilton Ave, Cincinnati, OH 45231 (513) 522-3860
Cincinnati Museum of Art, Eden Park Dr, Cincinnati, OH 45202 (513) 721-5204
Music Hall
Westwood Town Hall, 3017 Harrison Ave., Cincinnati, OH 45211-5701, (513) 662-9109

JEFFERSON CO.
Steubenville Public Library, 407 S. 4th St., Steubenville, OH 43952-2942 (614) 282-9782

KNOX CO.
Kenyon College, College Park St., Gambier, OH 43022-9623 (614) 427-5000

LAKE CO.
Rider's 1812 Inn, 792 Mentor Ave, Painesville, OH 44007 (440) 354-8200

LUCAS CO.
Linck Inn, 301 River Rd, Maumee, OH 43536 (419) 893-2388
Collingwood Arts Center, 2413 Collingwood Blvd, Toledo, OH 43620-1153 (419) 244-ARTS
Columbian House, 3 N. River Rd, Waterville, OH 43566, (419) 878-3006

MEDINA CO.
Hinckley Library, 1634 Center Rd., Hinckley, OH 44233-9485 (216) 278-4271
Intersection of St. Routes 303 and 94

MONTGOMERY CO.
Dayton Masonic Temple, 525 W. Riverview Ave. (937) 224-9795 TOURS BY AP-POINTMENT ONLY
Elinor's Amber Rose, 1400 Valley St, Dayton, OH 45402 (937) 228-2511
Englewood Dam. Route 40, through Englewood Reserve, National Road, Englewood, OH 45322-1337
Frankenstein's Castle, Patterson Ave, Hills & Dales Park
The Old Courthouse, 7 N Main St, Dayton, OH 45402 (937) 228-6271
Patty's House, Old National Trail Riding Center, 930 Patty's Rd, Englewood, OH 45377. Park at the stable parking lot, then turn left out of the parking lot and walk about 100 yards up the road until you see a dirt road blocked by posts. Walk up that road to the hanging tree and house site.
Sinclair Community College, 444 W. Third St, Dayton, OH 45402 (937) 226-2500
Sorg Opera House, 206 S. Main St, Middletown, OH (937) 422-2583
United States Air Force Museum, Springfield Street, Gate 28-B, Wright-Patterson AFB, Dayton, OH, accessible from 675 South or 75 South, (937) 255-3284
University of Dayton, 300 College Park Ave, Dayton, OH 45409 (937) 229-4114
Woodland Cemetery, 118 Woodland Avenue, Dayton, OH 45409 (937) 222-1431

MORGAN CO.
McConnelsville Opera House Theatre, 15 W. Main St, McConnelsville, OH 43756

OTTAWA CO.
Johnson Island Cemetery, island accessible from a causeway across Sandusky Bay from Bay Shore Rd.
Ottawa National Wildlife Refuge, off Rts 2 and 590, Oak Harbor, OH (419) 898-0014

PERRY CO.
Otterbein Cemetery, Rt. 22 out of Somerset

PIKE CO.
Pike Lake State Park, 1847 Pike Lake Rd, between US 50 and SR 124 (614) 493-2212

PREBLE CO.
Ft. St. Clair, follow signs on Rt. 122 or 732 out of Eaton

RICHLAND CO.
Malabar Farm/Ceely Rose House, Malabar Farm State Park, Pleasant Valley Rd, off Rt. 95 near the junction of 95 and 603 in Richland County (419) 892-2784
Mohican State Park, Rt. 3 just north of Rt. 97, Loudonville (419) 994-4290or 1-800-472-6700

ROSS CO.
The Majestic Theatre, 45 East 2nd St, Chillicothe, OH 45601-2543, (740) 772-2041

SUMMIT CO.
Goodyear Airship Operations, 841 Wingfoot Lake Rd, Mogadore, OH 44260

TRUMBULL CO.
Warren City Hall, 391 Mahoning NW, Warren, OH 44483-4634

VAN WERT CO.
Woodlawn Cemetery, 10968 Cemetery Rd., Van Wert, OH 45891 (419) 238-9564, to the right of Rt. 118 as you enter Ohio City, eight miles south of Van Wert

VINTON CO.
Hope Furnace, in Lake Hope State Park, Rt. 278 five miles north of Lake Hope, Zaleski, OH 45698, (740) 596-5253

WARREN CO.
Glendower State Memorial, 105 Cincinnati Ave., Lebanon, OH (513) 932-5366 or (937) 932-1817
Waynesville, on Rt. 42

WASHINGTON CO.
The Buckley House, 332 Front St., Marietta, OH 45750 (740) 373-3080
The Castle, 418 Fourth St., Marietta, OH 45750 (740) 373-4180
Lafayette Hotel, 101 Front St., Marietta, OH 45750 (740) 373-5522

WILLIAMS CO.
Nettle Lake, NW corner of Williams County, near the Michigan border, between 575 Rd and 475 Rd.

WOOD COUNTY.
Bowling Green State University, Bowling Green, OH 45403 (419) 372-2222

BIBLIOGRAPHY
More Ghostly Guide Books

Many of these books are available at my online catalog at http://www.invink.com. The emphasis here is on books with locations open to the public or books associated with ghost tours.

Adams III, Charles J., Cape May Ghost Stories, Vol. 2, *Reading, PA: Exeter House, 1997*

— *New York City Ghosts*, Exeter House, 1996. Charles J.Adams III is the prolific author of many more regional ghost books, particularly on New Jersey and Pennsylvania. Please check our web site for details.

—*Pennsylvania Dutch Country Ghosts, Legends and Lore*, Reading, PA: Exeter House, 1994

—*Philadelphia Ghost Stories, Chilling, True Stories of Haunted Places in the Most Historic City in America*, Reading, PA: Exeter House, 1998

Alexander, John, *Ghosts: Washington's Most Famous Ghost Stories*, Washington, D.C.: Washington Book Trading Company, 1975

Arnold, Melissa, *The Hauntings of Ellicott Mills*, Ellicott City, MD: Inch-by-Inch Enterprises, 1998

Bielski, Ursula, *Chicago Haunts: Ghostly Lore of the Windy City*, Chicago: Lake Claremont Press, 1997

Blackman, W. Haden, *The Field Guide to North American Hauntings*, New York: Three Rivers Press, 1998

Blue & Gray Magazine Editors, *A Guide to the Haunted Places of the Civil War*, Columbus, OH: Blue & Gray Magazine, 1996

Boye, Alan, *A Guide to the Ghosts of Lincoln*, Eugene, OR: Saltillo Press, 1987

Brooks, J.A., *Britain's Haunted Heritage*, London: Jarrold, 1991

—*The Good Ghost Guide*, London: Jarrold, 1994

Cain, Suzy, *A Ghostly Experience: Tales of Saint Augustine Florida*, St. Augustine: Tour St. Augustine, 1997

Cartmell, Connie, *Ghosts of Marietta*, Marietta, OH: River Press, 1996

Citro, Joe, *The Vermont Ghost Guide*, Hanover, NH: University Press of New England, 2000. Joe Citro is a popular Vermont writer on the paranormal. Check our web site for his other books including *Passing Strange* and *Green Mountain Ghosts*.

Collins ghost hunters' guide to Britain, London: Collins, 2000

Colombo, John Robert, *Haunted Toronto*, Toronto: Hounslow Press ,1996

Courtaway, Robbi, *Spirits of Saint Louis: A ghostly guide to the Mound City's unearthly activities*, St. Louis: Virginia Pub. Co., 1999

Coventry, Martin, *Haunted Places of Scotland*, Musselburgh: Goblinshead, 1999

Crawford, Richard, *Uneasy Spirits: 13 Ghost Stories from Clermont County, Ohio*, Newport, KY: Rhiannon Publications, 1997

Davis, Jefferson Dale, *Ghosts, critters & sacred places of Washington and Oregon,* Vancouver, WA : Norseman Ventures, 1999

Emberg, Joan Dehle and Buck Thor Emberg, *Ghostly Tales of Tasmania,* Launceston, Tasmania: Regal, 1991

Erickson, Lori, *Ghosts of the Amana Colonies,* Weaver, IA: Quixote, 1988

Farwell, Lisa, *Haunted Texas Vacations: the complete ghostly guide,* Englewood, CO: Westcliffe Publishers, 2000

Felumlee, Gary, *Ghosts in the Valley! Ghost Lore of Muskingum, Morgan, Coshocton, Guernsey and Tuscarawas Counties, Ohio,* Baltimore, MD: Gateway Press, 1998. Order directly from the author at Gary Felumlee, Office 305, The Masonic Temple, North 4th St., Zanesville, OH 43701

Foreman, Laura, *Haunted Holidays,* Bethesda, MD: Discovery Communications,1999

Forman, Joan, *Haunted Royal Homes,* London: Jarrold, 1987

Garcez, Antonio R., *Adobe Angels: Arizona Ghost Stories,* Truth or Consequences, NJ: Red Rabbit, 1998. Antonio Garcez has written a whole series of ghost books on New Mexico and the west. Please check our web site for a complete list.

Grant, Glen, *Obake Files: Ghostly Encounters in Supernatural Hawaii,* Honolulu: Mutual Publishing, 1996

Green, Andrew M., *Haunted Inns and Taverns,* Buckinghamshire: Shire Publications Ltd., 1995

Gruber, Suzanne and Bob Wasel, *Haunts of the Cashtown Inn,* The Authors, 1998

Halpenny, Bruce Barrymore*, Ghost Stations, True Ghost Stories, volumes 1-VII,* Chester-le-Street, Co. Durham: Casdec Ltd., 1990-1995

Hapgood, Sarah, *500 British Ghosts & Hauntings,* London: Foulsham, 1993

Hauck, Dennis William, *Haunted Places: The National Directory, Ghostly abodes, sacred sites, UFO landings, and other supernatural locations,* New York: Penguin,1996

— *The International Directory of Haunted Places,* New York: Penguin, 2000

Hervey, Sheila, *Canada Ghost to Ghost,* Toronto: Stoddart Publishing, 1996

Hiatt, Robert R., *The Ghosts of Fort Sill,* The Author, 1989

Hitchcock, Jayne A., *Ghosts of Okinawa,* Crofton, MD: Shiba Hill Ltd., 1996

Holzer, Hans, *Hans Holzer's Travel Guide to Haunted Houses,* New York: Black Dog & Leventhal, 1999

Jacobson, Laurie and Marc Wanamaker, *Hollywood Haunted: A Ghostly Tour of Filmland,* Santa Monica: Angel City, 1994

Jones, Richard, *Walking Haunted London,* London: New Holland, 1999

Klein, Victor C., *New Orleans Ghosts,* New Orleans: Lycanthrope Press, 1993

Marimen, Mark, *School Spirit, Volume 1: College Ghost Stories of the East and Midwest,* Holt, MI: Thunderbay Press, 1998. Mark Marimen is also the author of the *Haunted Indiana* series.

Marsden, Simon, *The Haunted Realm,* London: Little Brown, 1998

Mason, John, *Haunted Heritage,* London: Collins & Brown, 1999

Mead, Robin, *Haunted Hotels: A Guide to American and Canadian Inns and Their Ghosts*, Nashville, TN: Rutledge Hill, 1995
—*Weekend Haunts: A guide to haunted hotels in the UK*, London: Impact, 1994
Moore, Joyce Elson, *Haunt Hunter's Guide to Florida*, Sarasota: Pineapple Press, 1998
Myers, Arthur, *The Ghosthunter's Guide: To Haunted Parks, Churches, Historical Landmarks & Other Public Places*, Chicago: Contemporary Books,1992
—*The Ghostly Gazetteer: America's Most Fascinating Haunted Landmarks*, Chicago: Contemporary Books,1990
—*The Ghostly Register: Haunted Dwellings, Active Spirits: A Journey to America's Strangest Landmarks*, Chicago: Contemporary Books, 1986
Nesbitt, Mark, *The Ghosts of Gettysburg, Spirits, Apparitions and Haunted Places of the Battlefield*, Volumes 1-IV, Gettysburg: Thomas Publications, 1991-98
Norman, Michael and Beth Scott, *Haunted America, Vol. 1*, New York: Tor, 1994
—*Historic Haunted America*, New York: Tor, 1995
Okonowicz, Ed, *Welcome Inn, Spirits Between the Bays: Vol. III*, Elkton, MD: Myst & Lace, 1995, Ed is a storyteller and prolific author of the "Spirits Between the Bays" series of DelMarVa ghost stories. See our web site for a complete listing.
Ogden, Tom, *The Complete Idiot's Guide to Ghosts & Hauntings*, New York: Alpha Books, 2000
Pitkin, David, *Ghosts of Saratoga County*, Utica: North Country, 1998
Reichley, John, The *Haunted Houses of Fort Leavenworth*, Ft. Leavenworth, KS: Ft. Leavenworth Historical Society, 1995
Reinstedt, Randall A., *Incredible Ghosts of Old Monterey's Hotel Del Monte*, Carmel: Ghost Town Publishing, 1980. Randall A. Reinstedt is a very prolific writer on California ghosts. See our web site for more fine titles by this author
Roberts, Nancy, *America's Most Haunted Places*, Orangeburg, S.C. : Sandlapper Pub., 1987. Nancy Roberts is a storyteller and author of many books on Southern ghosts. You'll find a complete selection on our web site.
—*Georgia Ghosts*, Winston-Salem, SC: John F. Blair, Publisher, 1997,
—*Haunted Houses, Chilling Tales from 24 American Homes*, Old Saybrook, CT: Globe Pequot, 1998
Robson, Ellen, Dianne Halicki, *Haunted Highway: The Spirits of Route 66*, Phoenix, AZ: Golden West Publishers, 1999
Scott, Beth and Michael Norman, *Haunted Heartland*, New York: Warner, 1994
—*Haunted Wisconsin*, Sauk City, WI.: Stanton & Lee, 1980
Senate, Richard, *Ghost Stalker's Guide to Haunted California*, Richard Senate, Ventura: Charon Press, 1998. Richard Senate is a California ghosthunter with a long list of books. Please visit our web site for a complete listing.
Sharp, Eleyne Austen, *Haunted Newport*, Newport, RI: Austen Sharp, 1999
Sloan, David L., *The Ghosts of Key West*, Key West, FL: Phanton Press, 1998
Smith, Barbara, *Ghost Stories of Alberta*, Renton, WA: Lone Pine Publishing, 2000
—*Ghosts of Hollywood*, Renton, WA: Lone Pine Publishing, 2000. Barbara Smith

has a whole series of other books on Canadan and US ghosts. Please check our web site for details.

Spencer, John and Anne, *The Ghost Handbook*, London: Boxtree, 1998

Taylor, Jr., L.B., *The Ghosts of Virginia*, Volumes 1-IV Williamsburg: Progress Printing Co., 1993-98

—*The Ghosts of Williamsburg and Nearby Environs*, Williamsburg: Progress Printing Co., 1983

—*Virginia's Ghosts, Haunted Historical House Tours*, Alexandria, VA: Casco Communications, 1995

Thompson, Bill, *Lighthouse Legends and Hauntings*, Kennebunk, ME: Scapes Me, 1998

Underwood, Peter, *The A-Z of British Ghosts, An illustrated guide to 236 haunted sites*, London: Chancellor, 1992, (originally published as *Gazetteer of British Ghosts*)

—*Ghosts and How to See Them*, London: BCA/Anaya Publishers, 1993

—*Peter Underwood's Guide to Ghosts & Haunted Places, Cases from the files of the world's leading paranormal investigator*, Peter Underwood, London: Piatkus 1996

Upton, Kyle, *Niagara's ghosts at Fort George*, Newmarket, ONT: Kyle Upton, 1999

Weinberg, Alyce T., *Spirits of Frederick*, Braddock Heights, MD: A.T. Weinberg, 1992

Weird New Jersey, Mark Sceurman and Mark Moran. A fascinating (and weird) magazine published in May and October. www.weirdnj.com

Wilson, Alan, *Hidden & Haunted: underground Edinburgh*, Edinburgh: Mercat Tours, 1999. Visit their tour site at http://www.mercat-tours.co.uk/index.html.

Wilson, Patty, *The Pennsylvania Ghost Guide, Vol. 1*, Waterfall, PA: Piney Creek Press, 2000

Wlodarski, Robert J., Anne Nathan-Wlodarski, Richard Senate *A Guide to the Haunted Queen Mary*, West Hills, CA: G-HOST Publishing, 1995

Wlodarski, Robert J., Anne N. Wlodarski, Michael J. Kouri, *Haunted Alcatraz, A History of La Isla de los Alcatraces and Guide to Paranormal Activity*, West Hills, CA: G-HOST Publishing, 1998

Wlodarski, Robert and Anne, *The Haunted Whaley House*, West Hills, CA: G-HOST, 1997

—*Southern fried spirits: a guide to haunted restaurants, inns, and taverns*, Plano, TX: Republic of Texas Press, 2000

—*Spirits of the Alamo*, Plano, TX: Republic of Texas Press, 1999

Wood, Ted, *Ghosts of the Southwest: The Phantom Gunslinger and Other Real-Life Hauntings*, New York: Walker, 1997

—*Ghosts of the West Coast, The Lost Souls of the Queen Mary and Other Real-Life Hauntings*, New York: Walker, 1999

Zepke, Terrance, *Ghosts of the Carolina Coast: Haunted Lighthouses, Plantations and Other Sites,* Sarasota, FL: Pineapple Press,1999

Zullo, Allan, *The Ten Creepiest Places in America*, Mahwah, NJ: Troll, 1997

REFERENCES

Chapter One – **One Thousand Souls**
   [1] See the Avalon web site for a full report on OSR: http://www.alliancelink.com/users/avalon/mansfield.htm

Chapter Two – **Phantoms at the Folly**
   [1] *Uneasy Spirits, 13 Ghost Stories from Clermont County, Ohio*, Richard Crawford, Rhiannon Publications, 1997, p. 35

Chapter Three – **Ghosts at the Sign of the Golden Lamb**
   [1] *The Golden Lamb*, Hazel Spencer Phillips, Oxford, OH: The Oxford Press, 1993
   [2] *Henry Clay: Statesman for the Union*, Robert V. Remini, NY: W.W. Norton, 1991, p. 113

Chapter Four – **Portrait of a Lady**
   [1] "Taft Museum, 60th Anniversary, 1932-1992," *Cincinnati Magazine*, November 1992
   [2] "The Fine Art of Haunting," Owen Findsen, *Cincinnati Enquirer,* 31 Oct. 1991, C-1, C-2. Used with permission from *The Cincinnati Enquirer*/Owen Findsen."

Chapter Six – **The Pool Room**
   [1] *Toledo Blade*, 17 May, 1859

Chapter Seven – **Back! By Popular Demand!**
   [1] *Ghosts of Marietta,* Connie Cartmell, Marietta: River Press, 1996, p. 25

Chapter Nine – **Spooks at Spitzer**
   [1] See the Avalon web site for a full report on Spitzer House: http://www.alliancelink.com/users/avalon/spitzer.htm

Chapter Eleven – **Three Eerie Pieces**
   The Ghost of Captain "D" video, courtesy of William T. Hall, President, Central Ohio Fire Museum.

Chapter Thirteen – **My Otherworld and Welcome To It: Thurber House, Columbus**
   [1] Quoted in *The Thurber House Organ*, Autumn 1988, (Vol. 6 No. 2) "The Ghost Issue", p.
   [2-6] Ghost fact sheet provided by Thurber House, 2000
   [7] "Haunted by HALLOWEEN." Laurie Hertzel, [Minneapolis-St. Paul] *Star Tribune*, 30 Oct. 1996 1E

Chapter Fifteen - **The City of the Dead**
   [1] *Ancient Monuments of the Mississippi Valley,* E.G. Squier and E H Davis, 1848

Chapter Eighteen –**Esprit de Corps**
   [1-2, 4-5] Ghost story sheet provided by Mr. Tesch
   [3] *A brief sketch of the Cleveland Grays; outlining a few of the principal happenings during a period of sixty-six years*, George W. Tibbits, 1902

Chapter Twenty-two – **Two Spirited Women**
   [1] "The Kelton House: A Sad Tale of Insanity and Death," *Blue & Gray magazine*, Vol. XV, Issue 1 (Fall 1997), p. 51

Chapter Twenty-three – **The Undertaker's Revenge**
   [1, 6-7] *Ironton Tribune*, 5 July 1933
   [2-3] *Ironton Tribune*, 25 May 1933
   [4] *Ironton Tribune*, 14 June 1933
   [5] *Ironton Tribune*, 3 July 1933
   [8-9] *Ironton Evening Tribune*, 6 July 1933
   [10] *The Coffin with the Plate Glass Front or The Undertaker's Revenge*, Jean Dolan, Ohio Valley Folk Research Project, Chillicothe: Ross County Historical Society, 1960, New series #49
   [11] *The History of Woodland Cemetery, Ironton, Ohio*, Written and Compiled by Naomi Deer, The Author, n.d.

Chapter Twenty-four – **Blessed are the Poor in Spirit**
   [1] All historical material in this chapter comes from *The Home: The History of the Wood County Infirmary*, Craig Wismer, Bowling Green: Wood County Historical Society, 1997

and *The Home: A Tour of the Wood County Historical Museum,* Bowling Green: Wood County Historical Society, n.d. as well as communications from the Wood County Historical Center staff. I am grateful to them for their help.

[2-3, 5] "Spooky Halloween Tales from the Old County Home," Tales compiled by Tanya Hedges, Intern, Wood County Historical Center, Bowling Green: Wood County Historical Society, 1999

[4] *Everyday Life in the Wood County Infirmary,* Lucy Long, Unpublished ms., 1986. Located at Center for Archival Collections, Bowling Green State University, Bowling Green, OH 43403

INDEX

INDEX OF STORIES BY LOCATION

NOTE! *PLEASE DO NOT TEAR OUT THIS PAGE. XEROX THIS FORM OR COPY YOUR ORDER ONTO A SHEET OF PAPER.*

HOW TO ORDER YOUR OWN AUTOGRAPHED COPIES OF THE *HAUNTED OHIO* SERIES
Visit our web site at www.invink.com

Call **1-800-31-GHOST (1-800-314-4678)** with your VISA or MasterCard order or send this order form to: **Kestrel Publications, 1811 Stonewood Dr., Dayton, OH 45432 • Fax: (937) 320-1832**

_____ copies of **GHOST HUNTER'S GUIDE** @ $14.95 ea. $_____

_____ copies of **SPOOKY OHIO** @ $8.95 each $_____

_____ copies of **HAUNTED OHIO** @ $10.95 each $_____

_____ copies of **HAUNTED OHIO II** @ $10.95 each $_____

_____ copies of **HAUNTED OHIO III** @ $10.95 each $_____

_____ copies of **HAUNTED OHIO IV** @ $10.95 each $_____

_____ **Ghost Hunter's Guide** T-shirt @ $16.00 each $_____
(full color)
Size ____M ____L ____XL ____XXL ____XXXL

_____ **Spooky Ohio** T-shirt @ $14.00 each $_____
Size ____M ____L ____XL ____XXL ____XXXL

_____ **Haunted Ohio** T-shirt @ $14.00 each $_____
Size ____M ____L ____XL ____XXL ____XXXL

+ $2.50 Book Rate shipping, handling and tax for the first item, $1.00 postage for each additional item. Call (937) 426-5110 for speedier mail options. $_____

                                                TOTAL $_____

NOTE: We usually ship the same or next day. Please allow three weeks before you panic. If a book *has* to be somewhere by a certain date, let us know so we can try to get it there on time.

MAIL TO (Please print clearly and include your phone number)

_____

_____

FREE AUTOGRAPH!

If you would like your copies autographed, please print the name or names to be inscribed. _____

PAYMENT MADE BY:
☐ Check ☐ MasterCard ☐ VISA
($15 min. order on credit cards)

Card No. _____ Expiration Date:

Signature _____ Mo____ Yr _____